START & RUN A CRAFT BUSINESS

William G. Hynes

Self-Counsel Press
(a division of)
International Self-Counsel Press Ltd.
USA   Canada

Self-Counsel Press acknowledges the financial support of the Government of Canada through the Book Publishing Industry Development Program (BPIDP) for our publishing activities.

Printed in Canada.

First edition: 1984
Second edition: 1986
Third edition: 1990
Fourth edition: 1992; Reprinted: 1992
Fifth edition: 1993; Reprinted: 1993; 1994 (2); 1995
Sixth edition: 1996; Reprinted: 1999
Seventh edition: 2001; Reprinted: 2005

Cataloguing in Publication Data

Hynes, William G.
    Start & run a craft business

    (Self-counsel business series)
    Previous eds. have title: Start and run a profitable craft business
    ISBN 1-55180-372-0

    1. Handicraft — Management.   2. Handicraft — Marketing.   3. Selling — Handicraft
I. Title. II. Series
HD2341.H95 2001   745.5'068   C2001-911518-0

Self-Counsel Press
(a division of)
International Self-Counsel Press Ltd.

1704 North State Street   1481 Charlotte Road
Bellingham, WA 98225   North Vancouver, BC V5J 1H1
USA   Canada

CONTENTS

PREFACE

Since its first appearance, *Start & Run a Craft Business* has gone through numerous editions and reprintings, and I have received much positive feedback from fellow craftspeople. I now feel justified in my initial assumption that the book's generalist approach would be useful to the beginner as well as the more established craftsperson. When the book was first published, there were very few books available about the business side of craft making. Since then, numerous other books on crafts have appeared, some focusing on particular aspects of business as they relate to crafts, others concentrating on the techniques of the various individual crafts.

This book continues to be unique in that it provides a kind of overall blueprint for starting and running a craft business. No matter in what particular medium a craftsperson works, or on what scale he or she wishes to operate, this book provides detailed advice on how to proceed. It covers all the important areas of craft business for the part-time, single-person operation as well as the larger factory type or cottage industry craft business. It also looks in detail at the issues and problems involved in expanding a small craft business into a larger operation.

In the present edition, I have expanded the book to include a new chapter on selling crafts on the Internet. I have also added much new information throughout the book. There have been many changes in the North American economy in recent years, but one thing has not changed: the popularity of handcrafted products continues to grow. According to a recent survey by the Craft Organization Directors' Association, the fine crafts market is worth approximately $14 billion dollars annually to the American economy.

The number of men and women starting up craft businesses has also grown greatly. While in some cases this has led to increased competition among craftspeople, craft businesses continue to flourish throughout North America. This is partly due to the growing appreciation of handcrafted products by a public that has become increasingly knowledgeable of and educated about crafts. Continued popularity of handcrafts has led to a general rise in craft standards. The quality of today's Canadian and American handcrafts is higher than ever before.

In recent years, mass-market producers have tried to cash in on the growing popularity of handcrafts by copying craft designs and turning out vast quantities of cheap imitations. This is seen as a problem by some craftspeople, but others regard it as a challenge and an opportunity to widen the market for genuine handcrafted products.

What is certain is that these challenges and opportunities point toward an exciting future for craft businesses in the years ahead.

Chapter 1

THE ADVANTAGES OF A CRAFT BUSINESS

A successful craft business can be started and operated by almost anyone who is prepared to follow the suggestions in this book. If you are already involved in crafts as a hobby, you have a good head start, but even if you have never produced a handcrafted product, you can still learn to set up and operate a successful craft business.

One man, bored and frustrated with a dead-end job, turned his woodworking hobby into a profitable business that now provides full-time employment for himself and an assistant.

A homemaker and mother of two small children wanted to do something in addition to looking after her children. She did not want to go to work for someone else, especially since she had no specific job training except as a secretary, a job she had always disliked.

Then one day she had a brilliant idea. She had always enjoyed designing and making clothes for her own children, and she thought that just for fun she would try selling some of her work in a local craft market. Two years later, she had built up a successful part-time business making handcrafted children's clothes. Her part-time business brings in more money than she earned as a full-time secretary, and it allows her to be at home with her children as well.

CRAFTWORKERS ARE

MADE, NOT BORN.

These two people love their work and, by properly organizing the business side of their crafts, they are making good profits at the same time. What more could a person want?

There are several hundred thousand craftworkers in the United States and Canada. These people range from individuals who earn extra income from their part-time businesses to designers/craftspeople who own and manage substantial companies and direct the work of highly skilled employees.

The technical efficiency of our modern society and its cheap, mass-market products with their built-in obsolescence has created a large and growing consumer craving for finely wrought, individually produced, handmade products. Each year, billions of dollars worth of handcrafted products are sold in North America and the market is growing rapidly.

Most of these products are made by individual craftworkers and small- to medium-size craft companies. Most of these craftspeople work out of their own homes. They usually started their craft businesses in their spare time, so there was no need for them to give up their jobs until their businesses were off and running.

This is one of the biggest advantages of a craft business — that it can be started at home in your spare time. There is no need to invest in a costly plant and equipment. Most handcrafted products are made with the simplest of tools and equipment that rarely cost more than a few hundred dollars — and in many cases, much less.

Your initial workplace can be your garage, basement, or even your kitchen. Most crafts are relatively clean and quiet, involving no personal health or environmental hazards. The level of skill required varies widely, but most craft skills can be easily acquired by a person of average intelligence and manual dexterity.

Craftworkers are made, not born. In the past, they learned from their parents, and skills were often handed down from generation to generation. Today, most craftspeople learn their skills through practice, by taking craft courses, or from a friend.

Large numbers of people are already good amateur craftworkers. Think of the vast number of men and women who make, usually as a hobby or a way of saving money, handcrafted sweaters, socks, furniture, toys, and thousands of other items. These people may not think of themselves as craftworkers, though they already have many of the skills required to start a successful craft business.

Even if you are not making anything now, you can still train yourself as a craftworker. The list of possible handcrafted products is so extensive and the levels and types of skills required so varied that it is hard to imagine anyone who is not capable of making something handcrafted and, with the help of this book, turning it into a marketable product.

In fact, this book will show you how to start no matter what stage you have already reached. It covers topics such as —

(a) acquiring the skills you need,

(b) identifying a marketable product,

(c) setting up a production crafts workshop, and, above all,

(d) making your business profitable to achieve financial independence.

The value of financial independence has never been greater. Inflation, high unemployment, and general economic uncertainty are going to be with us in the foreseeable future. Rapidly changing technology is making many jobs redundant, and more and more people are succumbing to a feeling that their lives are being altered by economic forces they can neither understand nor control.

A craft business can give you a great measure of personal independence. You can be free of the nine-to-five grind, the pressures of cranky bosses and unpleasant coworkers, and the constant threat of layoffs. You can be your own boss and set your own working hours and conditions. You can make substantial profits.

Another big advantage to a craft business is that it is almost totally recession-proof. This is partly because handcrafts are high-quality, durable goods and, equally important, they are perceived by the public to represent quality and durability. Consequently, crafts are seen to be exceptionally good value for money. This helps keep sales up even in times of recession. In addition, the relatively small size and unique flexibility of craft businesses allows them to adapt to changing conditions more quickly and easily than most other kinds of business.

In addition to all this, a craft business gives you the chance to express yourself creatively, turning out high-quality, aesthetically appealing products.

A CRAFT BUSINESS CAN GIVE YOU A GREAT MEASURE OF PERSONAL INDEPENDENCE.

But you don't have to be a creative genius to start a craft business. In fact, you don't even need to be particularly creative. Many successful craftworkers produce all their work according to traditional designs. Others modify traditional designs to serve their own purposes.

You can produce hundreds or thousands of "production line" crafts (i.e., multiple copies) of the same design. Or you can concentrate on making one-of-a-kind craft pieces, where each piece is a unique design. There are good markets for both kinds of products in just about any craft medium. Whether you want to work in wood, clay, fiber, glass, or any one of hundreds of natural or synthetic materials, the markets for good-quality handcrafted products are large and growing.

What about business experience? Perhaps you feel more confident of your craft skills than your ability to market your work, to deal with the business side of things. What if you have no business experience at all?

Some of the most successful craftspeople around started out with little or no knowledge of business. Many of them even felt that they were not really "business types." Craftspeople come from the most diverse backgrounds. They are former teachers, plumbers, office workers, truck drivers, nurses, homemakers, just to mention a few. Most had no previous business experience and few would lay claim to any inborn "business sense."

What these people had was the desire and the determination to succeed. Most of them learned about business by actually doing business. In the beginning they made mistakes. But these were the kind of mistakes from which they could easily recover, then go back and do things right the next time.

This is another big plus in starting a craft business. You start out small, so that your mistakes are on a small scale. But if you start a craft business today, you probably won't make very many mistakes at all.

This is because times are better than ever for starting a craft business. Anyone starting out today has the benefit of the knowledge and experience of those who have gone before. The pioneers of the craft movement had to learn the hard way. In the early days there were no books like this on craft businesses. The only business books available were theoretical treatises written by academics and books on other types of business that had little or nothing to do with crafts.

The Internet has also created new opportunities for craftspeople. More and more of them are going online in search of information on techniques and new product ideas, to find suppliers, or to market their work.

Are there the same opportunities in crafts today as there were a decade or two ago? Isn't there a lot more competition these days? Yes, it is true there are a lot more craft businesses out there. There are also vastly greater opportunities than ever before because the growth of craft businesses in North America has expanded and increased the public's awareness of and demand for handcrafted products. As public demand has increased, so has the number of opportunities for craftspeople. One side of the equation fuels the other and there is no end in sight to this exciting trend.

Chapter 2

HOW TO GET STARTED

Perhaps you are already making handcrafted products as a hobby and you want to turn your hobby into a business. Or perhaps you have had no previous involvement in crafts, but have experience in some other kind of business. Either way, you have already acquired some of the knowledge and skills necessary to set up a successful craft business.

But what if you have never made anything handcrafted? What if you have had no previous business experience of any kind? What are your chances of successfully setting up and operating your own craft business?

Your chances are as good as anyone else's. If you are prepared to work hard at mastering the techniques of your chosen craft and if you go about the business side of it in a professional way, you are almost certain to succeed.

a. What to Make

Even if you have no previous experience in crafts, you may have definite ideas about what interests you. If certain types of handcrafted products have a special appeal to you, or if you feel that you have a special flair for something, that's the obvious place to start. You may

feel a strong attraction to a particular medium such as leather, stone, or wood. Perhaps you are interested in a particular field such as small gift items, clothing, toys, or tableware, but have no really clear idea about a medium. Wherever your interests lie, there are opportunities for selling your work in most of the traditional and contemporary craft fields.

If you have no previous craft experience and haven't the faintest idea of where to start, make a list of your skills or talents, your hobbies, and your job experience. You'll very likely discover that you are more versatile than you first thought.

Think of the things you've built in your basement workshop: the furniture for the children's rooms, the bookshelves you made last winter, and all the other bits and pieces you've made for the house. You've always liked working with wood in your spare time. With a little more experience, you could make almost anything in wood.

Or perhaps you enjoy knitting and crocheting and are pretty good at it. Think of all the things you make for the children or as Christmas gifts for friends and relatives. Why not try offering some of your fine handknitted sweaters for sale? You've seen similar products in craft shops at prices of anywhere from $100 to $250, and many of them were not half as nice as yours.

If you've never made anything at all, think of some of the things you'd like to make and try them out. Start out with what most interests you. If you think you'd like making jewelry or hooking rugs, then start there. Look around at craft markets and in craft shops for products you think you would like to make or learn to make.

Browse through some of the many craft books available. There are literally thousands of books on crafts and most likely your public library or a nearby bookstore has a good selection. If you don't have any particular craft in mind, then get one of the A to Z books on the various kinds of handcrafted products being made in North America. Look at both traditional and modern crafts.

The list in Table 1 gives you an idea of the possibilities. But don't limit yourself to this or any other list, because the possibilities are almost endless.

You can get good ideas for products to make by looking around in craft and gift shops and especially at craft shows. At craft markets, some booths attract large crowds and certain items appear to be "hotter" than others. One season it might be patchwork clothing or wind

START OUT WITH WHAT MOST INTERESTS YOU.

TABLE 1
LIST OF CRAFTS

Artwork
drawings
pictures
prints

Appliqué
aprons
pot warmers
T-shirts
wall hangings

Basketry
hats
plant hangers
mats

Batik
dresses
pillows
scarves
shirts
ties
wall hangings

Beadwork
bracelets
Indian beadwork
necklaces

Bookmaking

Calligraphy
journals
notebooks
calendars

Cartooning
caricatures
humorous
decorative

Ceramics
(greenware, stoneware, porcelain, ceramic tile)
bathroom accessories
bowls
brooches
butter dishes
cookie jars
cups
figurines
flower pots
fridge magnets
jugs
kitchen accessories
mugs
plates
pots
salt shakers
sculpture
sugar bowls
tiles
vases
wine coolers

Collage
installations
pictures

Crocheting
doilies
doll clothing
furniture covers
hats
tree ornaments
shawls

Doll making
porcelain dolls
rag dolls
period dolls

Dough art
animals
figurines
model buildings
tree decorations

Egg crafts
jewel boxes
knick-knacks
Ukrainian Easter eggs
Embroidery
clothing
cushions
furniture covers
pictures
purses
tapestries

Embroidery
clothing
cushions
furniture covers
pictures
purses
tapestries

Enamelling
jewelry
plates
trophies

Flower arranging
bouquets
wreaths

TABLE 1
Continued

Cooking and baking
bread
cakes
candy
cheese
chocolates
ethnic specialities
ice cream
preserves

Glass making
(blown, cut,
stained, etched)
bowls
figurines
goblets
lamps
mobiles
paper weights
sun catchers
tree ornaments
wind chimes

Graphic arts
decorative items
pictures
posters
T-shirts

Native crafts
beadwork
engraved silver
moccasins
featherwork

Kite making

Knitting
afghans
children's clothing
hats
mitts
socks
sweaters
pot holders
tree ornaments
vests

Lapidary arts
jewelry
paper weights
pen holders

Leather work
belts
book covers
book marks
briefcases
coats
eyeglass cases
footwear
gloves
hats
dog leashes and collars
knife sheathes
purses
saddlery
ties
vests
wallets
watch straps
wrist bands

Macrame
flowerpot holders
mats
wall hangings

Mask making
carnival masks
Halloween masks
theater masks

Metal working
(bronze, copper, gold,
iron, silver, pewter, steel)
barbecue sets
card holders
clocks
decorative ironwork
door knockers
fireplace sets
firewood holders
flower holders
gates
jewelry
knives
letter openers
lamps
light fixtures
napkin holders
picture frames
plates
puzzles
sculptures
trophies
weather vanes
wind chimes

TABLE 1

Continued

Musical instruments
door harps
fluteswood rhythm
    instruments

Papermaking
artist's paper
calendars
journals
lampshades
notepaper
writing pads

Patchwork
cushions
coats
eyeglass holders
jackets
placemats
potholders
purses
quilts
shopping bags
tablecloths
vests

Perfumes

Photography
animals
landscapes
old-fashioned
people

Plastic arts
decorative items
jewelry

Quilting
aprons
baby quilts
bed quilts
clothing
tote bags
wall hangings
rughooking
rugs
wall hangings

Sewing
aprons
children's clothing
coats
doll clothes
eyeglass cases
napkins
placemats
potholders
purses
shopping bags
tablecloths
tree ornaments
vests
wind socks

Scrimshaw
bookmarks
bracelets
earrings
key rings
paperweights
pendants
penholders

Shellwork
lamps
mobiles
ornaments
wreaths
tree decorations

Silk screen
clothing
scarves
wall hangings

Soap making
bath oil
bubble baths
gift packs
scented soaps
shampoos

Tapestry making

Tatting

Tole painting
decorative items
utensils

Toy making
folk toys
performing toys
stuffed toys
wooden toys
puzzles

Waxwork
candles
figurines
flowers
ornaments
tree decorations

TABLE 1
Continued

Weaving
- bed covers
- clothing
- children's clothing
- pillow covers
- placemats
- scarves
- wall hangings

Woodcarving
- animals
- decorative panels
- figurines
- relief carving

Wood turning
- bowls
- cups
- jewelry
- planters
- trophies
- vases

Woodworking
- bookcases
- breadboards
- cheeseboards
- cutting boards
- dollhouses
- doll furniture
- games
- jewelry
- picture frames
- puppets
- puzzles
- racks for cds
- signs
- toys
- trivets
- utensils

socks, porcelain figurines or bronze jewelry. Be careful not to let current fashions influence you too much in your choice of a medium or a particular product. On the other hand, don't be afraid to tackle something just because others are doing it if you think you can make it better or cheaper.

Look carefully at anything for which you feel a particular affinity. If you think you'd like the feel of potter's clay in your hands, then pottery may be your thing. Or perhaps you have welding experience and would like to work with metals. The best medium for you is the one with which you feel the strongest affinity.

Obviously, some crafts require more equipment than others. Perhaps you already have some of this equipment and experience using it. For example, you may already have a band saw or sewing machine and like using them, so this may determine your choice of a particular craft.

It is important to note in starting out in your craft business that some of the best-selling handcrafted products are often the simplest to make. You would be wrong to try making highly complex products at the beginning, no matter what medium you are in. As your skill and experience develop, you will soon be able to do the more advanced work and produce more sophisticated products. Even then you will often find, especially if you are in production crafts, that you are still selling a lot of basic things that are very simple and easy to make.

IN MOST CRAFT FIELDS, YOU CAN START MARKETING YOUR WORK WHILE YOU ARE LEARNING.

In fact, some of the best-selling crafts are so simple to make you might wonder at first glance if they are worth making at all. Take, for example, certain wooden toys, or fabric items like place mats. If people wanted a product this simple and easy to make, they would make it themselves, wouldn't they?

Actually, most of them wouldn't. This is because most people don't want to take the time and trouble to make something that they can buy from someone else. Craftspeople are successful in selling their products because they have taken the time and trouble to produce them and to produce them well — and because they know how and where to market them. This is where market research comes in, as we shall see in the next chapter. But first we need to take a look at ways of acquiring and upgrading your craftmaking skills.

b. How to Learn Craft Skills

Your goal is to achieve a mastery of the craft you have chosen. This is not something you will accomplish overnight. As your skills improve, you will set new challenges for yourself, and practicing your craft will become an ongoing learning process.

This does not mean that you must study and practice for years before you can sell any of your work. On the contrary, if you have chosen a field in which you are particularly adept, you can produce marketable work within a short time. In most craft fields, you can start marketing your work while you are learning. You will naturally produce simpler pieces first, following traditional or already-popular contemporary designs. You should not strive for too much originality at this point, but aim to master basic techniques.

Craft skills can be learned the same way most other skills are learned. There are a number of different ways of learning, none of which is inherently better than any other. Try the one that appeals most to you, or try them all.

1. Courses

Craft instruction is available in most large towns and cities. Formal craft study can range all the way from community evening courses at the local high school to the level of a university degree program. There are courses for beginners and advanced courses for experienced craftworkers. Some universities now offer a master's degree in crafts. Contact your regional, state, or provincial crafts organization for information on the availability of craft courses in your community. (See Appendix 2 for a list of national, state, and provincial craft organizations.)

But wait a minute, you say. I want to start making things, not go through a 12-month course, let alone a university crafts program. I want to set up a craft business, not enroll in a course of study.

There is a widespread belief today that you cannot really know anything about a subject unless you have taken a course in it. This is, of course, utter nonsense. Craft courses have a valid place in the learning process, but they are far from being the only route to mastery of a craft.

There's no reason why you have to complete a formal training course. Formal training in a craft, whether a single course or a whole program of courses, is in itself no guarantee that you will master the craft. Courses also have very little to do with the degree of commercial success you will have. Some of the best professional craftworkers around are entirely self-trained.

Whether or not you choose to take a craft course is very much a question of preference, depending partly on your own skills and partly on how you think you can best learn something new.

2. Apprenticeship

Perhaps you would rather work on a one-to-one basis with a professional craftworker. There are professional, working craftspeople who will provide apprenticeship training in their own studios. Some charge fees for the instruction, others offer training in return for help in their business. This can be an excellent way of learning about production as well as marketing and other aspects of a craft business.

Apprenticeship training can provide you with valuable insights into the nature of your craft that are almost impossible to get otherwise. If your instructor is really good, the creative inspiration you receive can have a major influence on your career. Your reputation can be greatly enhanced by having been an apprentice of someone who is widely known and respected in a particular field.

Unfortunately, opportunities for this kind of training are few. Most commercial craftworkers are too busy to provide training for an apprentice. Those who do usually accept only one apprentice at a time. Some craftworkers may be reluctant to provide training to someone whose main goal is to set themselves up in their own business in the same area.

NO MATTER HOW YOU GO ABOUT IT, YOU WILL LEARN MOST ABOUT YOUR CHOSEN CRAFT BY ACTUALLY DOING IT.

If you are interested in this kind of training, you may have to travel to another part of the country, but it's worthwhile if you get the opportunity to learn firsthand from a professional who is tops in his or her field.

Your local or regional crafts organization may have a list of the names of craftspeople who are willing to take on apprentices. Or, if you know a professional whose work you admire, you may want to approach him or her and ask to be taken on as an apprentice.

3. Teaching yourself

Perhaps you would rather teach yourself the skills you need. Many craftworkers have learned this way. Even if you have undergone formal training, you will find that the only way you can perfect the skills you have learned is by practice.

Books are an invaluable source of information on techniques, products, ideas, and markets, but don't just read. Try out the techniques and experiment with the methods described. You don't have to read a book from cover to cover for it to be of use to you. Get in the habit of using books to dig out just the specific information you require.

The Internet is another rich source of information on crafts, including product ideas, craft techniques, and outlets for your work. If you do not have your own computer or if you are not online, you can access the Internet at most public libraries.

c. Conclusion

No matter how you go about it, you will learn most about your chosen craft by actually doing it. Follow closely the techniques that you have read about or that you have learned from your instructor or craftworker friend. Don't expect to produce a masterpiece at the very outset. Chances are you'll spoil some materials in the beginning and make a bit of a mess without having a lot to show for it. Don't be discouraged. Keep trying.

If you've chosen something that you like, the learning process can be a lot of fun. As you progress, you'll be rewarded by the feelings of satisfaction and accomplishment that come from creating something.

You have now taken the first big step on the way to setting up your own craft business. The next chapter will tell you how to make things that will sell.

Chapter 3

HOW TO MAKE THINGS THAT WILL SELL

Whether you are teaching yourself or taking a course, you will experiment a lot on your own, testing new techniques, investigating new materials, and learning new skills. You will experience one of humanity's oldest and most deeply ingrained urges: the desire to create, to make with your own hands an object that has both an aesthetic and a functional value. Whether you're making hand-dipped candles or jade pins, the feeling of satisfaction from creating is the same.

This is all very fine, you say, but what about business? You're not making crafts just for the feeling of self-fulfillment that you get. You want to make some money at it too.

This is where you differ from most of the people who become casually involved with crafts. Most of those in your pottery or ceramics course, for example, want to make pots or paint figurines for relaxation or as a hobby. You are taking up pottery or ceramics with the intention of starting a business and selling your work at a profit.

Whether you're going to learn your craft as a pleasant way to pass the time or in order to make products to sell, you still have to master the basic techniques of the craft. There's no real difference there. The important difference between the professional and the hobbyist is in

the way you select and design the particular products you make. For example, if you're involved in woodworking as a hobby, you can make what you please. If you fancy making elaborate sideboards and other big pieces, that's fine. But if you plan to sell your work, you have to follow the market. You won't make any money producing big, one-of-a-kind items, no matter how nice they are, if people are chiefly interested in buying small, less expensive pieces like cheese boards or spice racks.

This applies no matter what stage you have reached in your craft career or what kind of products you are making. A number of friends of mine were formerly enthusiastic amateurs, producing work chiefly for their own pleasure, before they turned to crafts to make a living. In each case, they have had to substantially modify the items they produce in order to make their work marketable on a significant commercial scale.

In some cases, it may be necessary to make a radical change in the products you make if you want to be successful in the marketplace. This happened to Arthur and Betty Allthumbs. They started out by making elaborate pieces like sideboards and chests with carved oak panels. Their work was extremely impressive and beautifully done. It got a lot of attention at craft shows, but few buyers.

Arthur and Betty made numerous efforts to promote their work. They exhibited frequently, had brochures printed, and set off their displays with attractive props, including flowers, vases, and stuffed toys. Still, they sold only a few pieces here and there, not enough to make a living from their craft. Worse, from Arthur's point of view, was that people kept wanting to buy their "lovely" props, especially the stuffed toys that Betty made to advertise their work.

Finally, they realized they had been ignoring an excellent opportunity. Betty increased the number and variety of toys she made. It was not long before Arthur's carved chests and sideboards became booth fixtures for displaying the stuffed toy animals. Soon, Arthur joined forces with his wife to produce the new product line. Within a short time, the couple built up a substantial business producing handmade stuffed toys.

If you want to make any money selling your work, you must produce with your eyes fixed firmly on the market. You must have a quality product to begin with, but you must also produce what is marketable if you expect to make a living from your craft.

You don't usually have to go to the extreme of switching to a completely different medium as Arthur and Betty did. There will be a market for your work in virtually any of the main craft categories, provided you are producing the right product. But in order to do this, you first have to test the market.

a. Market Research

YOUR RESEARCH NEED NOT BE EXPENSIVE OR TIME-CONSUMING.

You may think market research is only for big companies with big budgets, while all you want to do is sell a few pots or handknitted sweaters. You can go ahead and sell a few pots or handknitted sweaters and not bother about researching the market. But if you really want to sell significant quantities of a product and make substantial profits, you have to know the market; that is, you have to know what people want to buy.

Your research need not be expensive or time-consuming. You will certainly find it worth the time and effort to find out what you can about potential markets before you start producing goods for sale.

Aim to find out as much of the following as you can:

(a) What are the possible retail outlets in your immediate area? (Look at chapter 8 on marketing for the different types of stores that carry handcrafted products.)

(b) Who are the typical customers of these shops? What are their approximate income levels? Are they mainly men or women? If, for example, you are producing clothing accessories like scarves and handbags, you would expect to be selling mainly to women.

(c) Is there a significant tourist trade in the area or do the stores cater chiefly to the area's residents? If tourists are important, try to think of products that may easily be identified with the area. For example, products with a nautical theme are usually popular with tourists in coastal areas.

(d) What kinds of prices are being paid for products similar to the ones you plan to make? How important a factor is price? A few handmade products are true luxury items and price is not a major factor in determining whether they will sell, but most products are more price sensitive.

(e) Is your type of product affected by fashion? Most clothing items are.

(f) How much competition is there? Have your competitors been around for long? If there is a lot of well-established competition, you may be better off staying away from that product and making something different.

(g) Who goes to the craft markets in your area and what do they buy? Find out where the best markets are (see chapter 5 on how to do this) and do a bit of reconnaissance, either on your own home turf or in a nearby town or city. It's not difficult to see what's selling at a craft market, there will be crowds around the busiest booths. Look around and ask yourself: Are the customers at these markets tourists passing through the area or are they locals? Are they rural types or office workers? What are their income levels? How are they dressed? Look in the parking lot to see what kinds of cars they drive.

(h) Are there differences among the different shows that you might attend? In our city, there are several major craft markets and each is distinctive in terms of the type of clientele it attracts. There is a market in the north end that draws a lot of people from the surrounding "blue-collar" areas, while another market in the south end pulls in executives and professionals. Also, since women buyers vastly outnumber men at all craft markets, it is imperative to have products that appeal to women, for themselves or as gifts for children and men.

(i) What about ideas for products that you don't see at all in shops or craft markets? If you have an idea for a product that no one seems to be selling, you may have a potentially "hot" item. Perhaps no one has thought of it before or no one has taken the trouble to make it. On the other hand, the absence of this product from shops and craft markets may be an indication that there is no demand for it. You may have to build a prototype of your product and test the market that way.

(j) If you are connected to the Internet, you should visit online craft shops and galleries to get ideas for products you might make. The Internet is a vast repository of information on crafts and craft marketing. (See Chapter 7 for detailed information on selling your crafts online.)

b. Market Test Your Products

Build prototypes of the products you plan to make and check your market research by actually testing your products in the market. You can use any of the marketing channels outlined in chapters 4 to 7 to do this, but selling your products at a craft market (covered in detail in chapter 5) is one of the best.

TRY TO FIND YOUR OWN PARTICULAR NICHE IN THE MARKET.

Selling at a craft market gives you firsthand experience with customers' reactions to your products. What do they think of the quality of your work? Are your prices considered to be high or low? Are they looking for work similar to yours but perhaps in slightly different sizes, styles, or colors?

Make prototypes using your existing facilities as much as possible, even if this means working on the top of the kitchen table in the beginning. Once you have discovered what is going to sell, you can start building up a stock of products, set up an adequate workshop, buy raw materials in bulk, and follow the other production techniques of a craft business as outlined in chapters 9 and 10. Don't put the cart before the horse and invest time, money, and effort in building up a stock of goods for which there is no market.

Try to find your own particular niche in the market. Look at what is selling in stores and at craft markets. Look at the quality and the prices. Concentrate on products that are in demand and that you can offer in a better design, quality, or price.

Say you are producing wooden toys and there are a lot of similar products in stores but they are almost all relatively large softwood toys. You may find a comfortable niche in the market by producing small, brightly painted hardwood toys for under $10.

Be careful to exhibit and offer for sale only your best work. Nothing travels faster than bad news, and you don't want your reputation to be based on premature work. If you are making production line crafts, one of the main skills you will develop is the ability to produce rapidly at a high standard of quality. But do not try to produce work quickly in the beginning.

Be prepared to follow the market and produce work for which there is a strong demand. The market for crafts is growing very quickly for those who are producing the right quality crafts. You will succeed if your work is of consistently high quality, if you follow the market to know what is selling, and if you know where to sell. Chapters 4 to 8 show you how to market your work.

BEFORE YOU SELL...

a. Wholesale or Retail?

Once you have identified and produced a marketable product, choosing your market is the most important decision you will make. Unless you can find markets, your work won't be sold, and while you may enjoy making crafts, you won't make any money and you won't be in business for long.

In marketing your work, you leave the ranks of the amateurs and become a true professional. This important transition is marked by a change in attitude toward your work. In the beginning, the objects you made were worthwhile because "you" made them, and you were naturally very proud of the fact. At the same time, you hoped that others would also find your work attractive. You might have shown the work to your craft instructor, a friend, or a fellow craftworker.

As a professional, you retain this basic pride in your work, but at the same time you come to regard the product less as an extension of yourself and more as an object in the marketplace. It is a beautiful object, to be sure, the result of your painstaking efforts, but you now come to see it as a high-quality, well-priced, marketable product.

Your task now is to take this product and sell it!

There are three basic ways you can go about selling your work. You can wholesale to shops, sell in stores on consignment, or retail your products directly to the public from your own studio, at craft fairs, through the mail, or on the Internet. Each method has its advantages and disadvantages. They are not mutually exclusive, and most successful craftworkers use a variety of wholesale and retail marketing channels.

1. Wholesaling

If you sell your work outright to stores, you get on average about half the final selling price. This is because most stores will mark up your goods by 100 percent; that is, they will sell your work at double the price you sell to them. This may seem excessive, but you must remember that retailers have big expenses, including high rents and taxes. If they are to be successful, they must be in a good location and spend money on advertising. No matter what they do, a certain amount of merchandise is always going to remain unsold and they have to absorb the loss.

It is possible to sell to shops on a strictly cash basis, but, as we shall see in a later chapter, this can hurt your sales if your competitors or other craftworkers are selling their goods on credit. In most cases, it will be necessary to offer your work on credit if you have any substantial amount of dealings with shops.

2. Consignment

It is possible to deal with some stores on a consignment basis. In this arrangement, the store does not actually purchase your work but agrees to put it on display and sell it for you. If you deal with a shop on this basis, you should get a higher proportion of the final selling price, between 60 percent and 70 percent, because the risk is yours, not theirs. If you deal on a consignment basis, you should have a written agreement with the shop (see the section on contracts in chapter 10).

You may be obliged to sell to shops on consignment at the beginning of your career. If your work is unknown, store owners may be unwilling to run the risk of outright purchase. However, as soon as your work becomes accepted in the marketplace, you should insist on a straight sale in dealing with most shops.

YOU MAY BE OBLIGED TO SELL TO SHOPS ON CONSIGNMENT AT THE BEGINNING OF YOUR CAREER.

Consignment is an unwieldy arrangement at best, as you never know exactly how much work you have sold until the retailer sends you your payment at the end of the month. Also, the retailer has less incentive to promote your work if he or she is looking at keeping only 30 percent or 40 percent of the price rather than the customary 50 percent retail markup, and is facing no loss if the piece doesn't sell.

Moreover, consignment involves considerably more paperwork than a straight sale. In addition to a written agreement with the consignee, you need to keep detailed records of how much of your stock is in the hands of the consignee at the end of each month.

3. Retailing

If you sell directly to the public, you receive all of the final selling price yourself. You make a profit as the producer of the goods and you make a profit again as the seller. However, before you start counting your profit, you have to reckon with selling expenses.

If you are selling at a craft market, the net income from sales can be relatively high. Sales from your own studio can also be more profitable than selling to stores. If you have your own separate retail outlet, you will have retail selling expenses, but you may still make more profit per sale than you would wholesaling.

Retailing all your work at craft markets will mean that you must spend substantial periods of time away from the workshop. This is seen as a plus by those who like traveling and/or meeting people. Even if you are not particularly fond of retail shows — and not all craftspeople are — it is still a good thing to meet your customers in person from time to time and get a first-hand idea of their reaction to your products.

Retailing your own work usually means going to shows or selling to the public out of your own studio. There are, however, a couple of other options. You can retail your work through the mail, something we consider in the following chapter when we look at the various selling channels in more detail. You can also take advantage of opportunities to sell your work on the Internet, a subject we explore in detail in Chapter 7.

4. Which is best for you?

The type of product you make and the quantities you produce will be the most important factors in determining whether you sell the bulk of your work to shops or directly to the public. If you are producing unique, one-of-a-kind items, it may be possible to sell all your work directly to customers, either through markets, from your own studio, through the mail, or on the Internet. If you are making production crafts on a part-time basis, it may also be possible to dispose of your entire output at retail. But if you are making production crafts full time and have a substantial output, you will probably want to do some wholesaling.

Even if you are able to sell most of your output at craft markets, wholesaling can be a valuable "second string" to your bow. If you are dealing with shops, you will have a smoother and more even cash flow as payments from stores will come in at times when you are not selling at shows. Selling to shops enables you to reach further afield than it might be practical for you to travel personally. Sales on the Internet also have this advantage. This, of course, does not rule out selling as much of your work as possible at craft markets or from your own studio. In fact, since you normally make a higher net profit per item on retail sales, you should aim to sell as high a percentage as possible of your output at retail.

Most craftworkers use a variety of marketing channels. Chapters 5 and 6 look at the traditional marketing channels in detail. Chapter 7 deals with new selling opportunities offered by the Internet.

MOST CRAFTWORKERS USE A VARIETY OF MARKETING CHANNELS.

b. Pricing Your Work

Pricing is very important. If your products are priced too low, you will undercut the market and end up working for nothing. On the other hand, if you put too high a price on your work, you will find your goods priced out of the market.

Set a wholesale price for your work first. If you are also selling your work at retail, simply add on an appropriate retail markup. (I discuss this below.) If you are selling the bulk of your work to shops, bear in mind that most shops will compute the selling price to the customer by doubling your wholesale price.

There are two basic ways you can go about setting wholesale prices for your work:

(a) Cost of production: Using this method, you determine all the direct and indirect costs of producing a piece. You add a certain amount over and above this as your profit and you have your wholesale selling price.

(b) What the market will bear: Using this method you look at what similar products are selling for in the marketplace and try to set your prices so that they are not too far above or below those of the main competition.

In practice, you will usually find that a combination of both methods works best.

Start out by calculating all your production costs or the costs of all your material and labor. Material costs should be fairly easy to calculate. Don't forget to allow a certain amount for waste, and remember to include all the materials you use.

Labor costs are a bit more difficult to determine, especially in the beginning stages of your career. Minimum wage rates or prevailing wage rates in your area are of little use to you when you are working for yourself. More important is the time it takes you to produce a price in relation to the time taken by an experienced craftworker. You certainly can't charge more for a piece simply because it takes you longer to produce it! On the other hand, you do not necessarily have to lower your prices as you become more efficient. As you gain experience, you will earn more per hour from your work.

After calculating your labor and material costs, you then determine your indirect or overhead costs and add a portion of these to the cost of each item you produce. You start by estimating your total overhead costs for a given period of time — usually a year. Be careful not to overlook anything. Think of heat, light, rent, telephone, office supplies, and postage. In addition to all these, include the time you spend managing the business, designing products, purchasing supplies, and selling. All these are very real business costs, and if you do not factor them into your selling price, you will be that much out of pocket.

When you have an estimate of your total yearly overhead costs, divide this figure by 12 to arrive at an estimate of your monthly overhead. Estimate as accurately as you can how many of each item you make per month and divide your monthly overhead figure by this amount. The result will be the amount that should be added to the cost of production of each item to cover your overhead.

Now you can add on your net profit figure. This will be the amount you want to clear on each item after you have paid for all the costs of production and overhead costs. You do not need to make the same percentage profit on each item. On some of your bigger, more expensive items you may not want as high a percentage markup as on some of the smaller items. On average, you should aim for a net profit in the range of 15 percent to 25 percent. Sample 1 shows how pricing would be done for Dandy Dolls.

Check your price calculations against the prices of similar work in shops. If your prices appear too high, you must go back to your cost of production figures and recalculate your profit percentages, reduce your hourly labor costs, or try to cut the costs of your raw materials, perhaps by bulk buying (see chapter 10). Alternatively, you may want to avoid selling to shops and instead concentrate your efforts on selling your work directly to the consumer.

AIM FOR THE HIGHEST POSSIBLE PRICE AT WHICH YOUR PRODUCT WILL SELL.

There are many successful craftspeople who never market through shops because their work will not sell once the wholesaler's markup is added on. In such cases it is possible to proceed directly to the second method of pricing; that is, charging what the market will bear. Even if you sell the bulk of your work at wholesale, it is a good idea to try out your prices at craft markets.

In selling directly to the public at craft shows, beginners are more likely to underprice than overprice their work. This is because they are determined to succeed and they often feel that their product will sell better if the price is low. Also, they are aware of the "flaws" in their work, the minor imperfections that are not noticed at all by the public.

You should try experimenting a bit in the beginning with prices. Look at the prices of competing goods or goods similar to your own and aim to come roughly half way between the highest and the lowest of these. If you sell everything very quickly, you should raise your prices gradually, though not so high that they hamper sales. If your initial prices don't attract a sufficient number of buyers, you will have to lower them. Aim for the highest possible price at which your product will sell.

Your net profit will usually be much higher when you retail your work at craft shows — as high as 50 percent to 80 percent, depending on the show costs and the costs of your material. This is certainly a good argument for selling as much of your work as possible at shows, even if you also have a large wholesale business.

A factor that is sometimes important in retail pricing is the consideration of various "price points," such as $10, $20, $50, above which, for some products, there may be a certain amount of consumer

PRICING WORKSHEET

MATERIAL COSTS

Fabric	$1.40	
Filling	.25	
Eyes	.12	
Felt accessories	.28	
Total material costs		$2.05

LABOR COSTS

Sewing	$1.05	
Filling	.15	
Closing	.25	
Finishing	.50	
Total labor costs	$1.95	

Total production costs		$4.00

Total overhead per month	$600.00	
Number of units produced per month	800	
Per unit overhead cost		.75
Total per unit cost		4.75

Net profit margin 20%		1.19*
Wholesale selling price		$5.94
Retail selling price		$11.88

---

*To calculate a 20% profit margin, proceed as follows:

80% of the wholesale price = $4.75 (i.e., your total cost per unit)

100% of the wholesale price = $4.75 ÷ 80 x 100 = $5.94

Profit margin = $5.94 − $4.75 = $1.19

hesitation. In such cases, it is often desirable to price a product just slightly below one of these points — for example, $4.75 or $4.95 rather than $5.

It is also important to be able to offer your customers a range of prices; that is, to have a product line with items in each of the main price ranges. Some people may be looking for an inexpensive gift under $5. Others may not be able to afford your large Number Ten Widget and instead settle for a medium-size Number Ten.

There are also differences among various craft markets in terms of what people can afford or are willing to pay. It is neither advisable nor ethical to adjust your prices upwards or downwards to suit a different clientele, but you can offer a range of products and prices for different types of customers. At Christmas time, we sell a lot of our less expensive toys at a market in the north end of the city in a predominantly working class area. At another market, in the "upscale" south end, a few weeks later, we sell quite a few of the more expensive items. When times are good, we sell more of our higher priced items than when times are not so good. It is best to be as versatile as possible and offer a range of products to appeal to different pocketbooks.

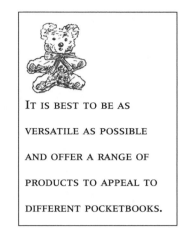

IT IS BEST TO BE AS VERSATILE AS POSSIBLE AND OFFER A RANGE OF PRODUCTS TO APPEAL TO DIFFERENT POCKETBOOKS.

c. Sales Literature

Whichever way you choose to sell your products, you will need sales materials that you can leave with undecided store owners, hand out at trade shows, or display in a craft show booth for people to pick up and take with them. Sales literature can be as simple as a business card or as elaborate as a color catalog with detailed descriptions of all the items in your line.

1. Business cards

Your business card should include your name, the name of your company, your business address, and your phone number. If you have e-mail and a Web site, it is important to include these on your business card. Your card should also include a brief description of your work (e.g., "Precious Gems" or "Custom Woodwork"). While you can order a fancy business card with your name in raised, gold-embossed lettering, it saves money and is just as effective if you pick a simple design. Business cards are very inexpensive when ordered in lots of 500 or 1,000 using one of the many available standard type styles.

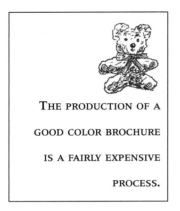

THE PRODUCTION OF A GOOD COLOR BROCHURE IS A FAIRLY EXPENSIVE PROCESS.

The cost may go up if you have pictures, drawings, or a company logo which requires the printer to do special artwork. If you have a computer, an ink-jet or laser printer, and desktop publishing software, you can easily print your own business cards using blank business card stock available in most office supply stores. Some word processing programs also have the capacity to print business cards.

2. Brochures and catalogs

Brochures and catalogs enable you to place information on your products in the hands of prospective customers. They can be a valuable sales tool whether you hand them out to prospective customers who visit your booth, send them out through the mail, or use them to show your products to store owners. This is the good side.

The bad side is that they are relatively expensive to prepare and to print. More than one craftsperson has had the experience of going to a great deal of time and trouble to prepare a color brochure only to be disappointed by the final result.

The production of a good color brochure is a fairly expensive process involving photography, design work, color separation, and printing. A black and white brochure is simpler and less expensive. Should you decide to go for a color brochure or even a black and white one, you should use a reputable design firm. If you pick one from the *Yellow Pages*, ask to see some examples of their work before you decide.

For most small craft businesses, the simplest and most cost-efficient brochure is a one-page information sheet that can be photocopied. With recent advances in photo reproduction, it is not difficult to make good quality copies of drawings and even pictures; however, you don't necessarily have to produce images. A listing of your products with brief descriptions, sizes, and prices will often be sufficient.

If you have desktop publishing software on your computer, you may want to produce your own brochure. Many advanced word processing programs also have the capability to produce a basic brochure. The decision to do the work yourself or to hire a professional will depend on the kind of brochure you want and how you plan to use it. If you really want an eye-catching, glossy brochure that will impress people who have never seen your actual products, you should use a professional service. However, if you just want something inexpensive that you can hand out to customers at craft shows, you might want to produce your own.

Chapter 5
RETAILING YOUR WORK

a. Retailing from Your Studio

If you retail your own products, you are entitled to include the retailer's markup in your selling price. In actual practice, however, most craftworkers will not charge the full retailer's markup on sales of their own work.

If you are selling directly to the public from your own workshop, your retail overhead costs should be relatively low. You may be better off taking less than the usual 100 percent retail markup. You will make a little less on each sale, but, because of your reasonable prices, you will sell more of your work and end up making more money.

However, if you are also selling to shops in the same general area as your studio, it may not be wise to sell your work for substantially less than they do. Some store owners will refuse to handle your work if you are undercutting them on the price. If you do not sell to any local stores, then you won't have this problem and you can set your retail prices without reference to shops. Of course, your work will still have to be priced competitively with similar work being sold in shops.

Location is the single most important factor in retailing. If your workshop is located in a busy shopping area — for example, a main

downtown thoroughfare or on a major tourist route — you may be able to sell a large part of your output right out of your own front door.

If you happen to be in a very good location for retailing, you might want to set aside a separate retail area in your workshop. You may even want to carry other non-competing crafts as well as your own work. Having different types of work can enhance the attractiveness of your shop and boost sales of your own work.

If you are not in a good location for retailing or if your studio layout or working hours do not lend themselves to retailing, you may be able to sell only a small proportion of your work from your own premises. Rather than trying to attract buyers to you, you may want to take your work to where the buyers are. A good way to do this is to sell your products in a craft market.

b. Retailing Your Work at Craft Markets

Craft markets have provided the launching pad for many successful craft businesses. Learning about craft markets can be a lot of fun and it is only by experience that you will learn all you really need to know about markets (or shows, as many craftspeople call them). However, there are some things you should know when starting out.

This section gives you important and valuable information on craft markets, such as how to —

    🦋 find craft markets,

    🦋 select the best ones,

    🦋 get accepted into the best ones,

    🦋 prepare for them, and,

    🦋 sell your work.

1. How to find craft markets

Craft shows are held in many different kinds of locations, from downtown convention centers and sports arenas to suburban shopping malls, parks, and even country fields. Some are organized by state and provincial arts councils or associations of craftspeople. Others are run by a variety of civic groups and voluntary organizations such as charities. However, the majority of shows are run by private promoters, who operate their shows as money-making ventures.

Many shows have some kind of jury system. In the case of many local and state craft organizations, participation in shows is restricted to members of the organization, though many have reciprocal arrangements with other organizations for members to attend each others' shows. The criteria for joining most of these organizations are similar to the criteria for getting your work accepted into shows.

Some shows have restrictive entry requirements, such as accepting only crafts of a certain type (e.g., metalwork), or on a certain theme (e.g., the Old West), or from a particular region. However, most shows accept a fairly broad range of handcrafted products in all the main categories.

There are so many craft shows that a complete listing of show organizers and their addresses in the u.s. and Canada would fill a large portion of this book. Information on many of the larger shows can be found in show directories, such as those listed in Appendix 1, which also contains the Web addresses of several searchable databases of craft shows. State and provincial craft organizations also frequently publish newsletters with information on craft shows in their area. (See Appendix 2 for a list of state and provincial craft organizations.) For local shows contact groups in your community, such as Chambers of Commerce and voluntary organizations, including charities, sports organizations, and church groups. Civic centers and craft supply stores may also know of local groups who sponsor craft shows.

It is a good idea for beginners to start out at one of the smaller local craft shows. Booth fees are generally less and, if the show is in your community, you do not need to incur expenses for travel and overnight lodging. Local shows are a good way to get a feel for the experience of selling at a craft market and to gauge how much demand there is for your products.

2. How to pick the best craft shows

There are so many shows available these days that it is necessary to be selective in deciding which to attend. Talking to other craftspeople is an excellent way of finding out about a show. It is important to remember, however, that shows produce different results for different people. Sometimes a woodworker will do extremely well at a show, while a potter at the same show will have disappointing results. Or one potter may have big sales while another potter's sales are only mediocre. There are so many variables at work that it is difficult to judge the potential for your work from the results obtained by others. As well, people do not always level with you where money is involved, so you cannot always take their comments at face value.

When assessing a show, ask the following questions:

- What is the quality of the other products being offered for sale? You don't want to damage your reputation by associating your work with low-quality shows, bazaars, secondhand sales, and flea markets.

- How well is the show promoted; that is, how much advertising is done by the organizers? In the best craft markets, a good proportion of the booth fee goes toward advertising: posters, newspapers, radio, and television should all be used to bring the show to the attention of the public. You certainly don't want to waste your time and money on markets for which there is insufficient advance publicity.

- Where is the craft market located? No matter how much advertising is done, large numbers of buyers won't be attracted unless the location is easily accessible and there is adequate (preferably free) parking.

- What time of year is the show being held? Generally speaking, fall shows provide much bigger sales than spring shows, and shows held in the pre-Christmas buying season are the best of all. This is not hard to understand if you realize that most retailers make 50 percent or more of their annual sales during the Christmas period. For certain kinds of products such as giftware, the percentage of annual sales in the Christmas period is even larger. So make the most of your opportunities to attend fall and Christmas shows.

(a) Mall shows

A busy shopping mall attracts large crowds and, at first glance, would appear to be a good location for a craft market. However, things are not always what they seem. In general, the shopping-mall crowd is much more diverse than the crowd that attends a traditional type of craft market. In other words, it is more representative of the public at large than the craft-show crowd, which usually has a high proportion of college-educated, middle- and upper-income buyers. Most of the shopping-center crowd have come to the mall for purposes that have nothing to do with the craft show, and many are looking for bargains and low-priced or discounted merchandise.

Mall shows have other drawbacks as well. They have long hours — sometimes up to 12 hours a day — and many require craft-show vendors to pay the promoter a commission (usually 10 percent or 15 percent) on sales in addition to the booth fee. Moreover, despite the claims of promoters, mall shows are usually not juried shows. So craftspeople will often find themselves alongside vendors of all kinds of mass-produced merchandise. And many of the vendors will be sales representatives who have not made the products they are selling.

This does not mean that mall shows are no good. There are plenty of craftspeople who do extremely well at mall shows. It depends to some extent on the particular kind of mall. The crowd that flocks to an upscale shopping center in an affluent neighborhood will be quite different from the crowd that is drawn to the average suburban mall. The kind of crafts being sold is also important. If you have products that appeal to a wide range of tastes and pocketbooks, you could do well at mall shows.

If you decide to enter a mall show, be prepared for long hours and remember that, unlike a traditional craft show, a mall show means that you are competing not just with other craftspeople, but with a whole variety of other goods and services as well.

(b) Other mall outlets

There are several variations of the mall show that have worked well for some craftspeople. Instead of a temporary booth for a few days or weeks (some mall shows run for up to a month), they rent a kiosk in a mall for a longer period of time. Or a mall promoter may rent or lease a mall store to a group of craftspeople who set up individual booths inside the store. These kinds of arrangements work especially well for some craftspeople in the weeks before Christmas when mall traffic is at its highest. They have more in common with running your own retail outlet than with the traditional craft market. Net return per item is usually less than in traditional craft markets because of the relatively high rental or leasing costs, but this can be more than offset by the large number of items you can sell in a busy shopping mall in the four to six weeks leading up to Christmas.

IF YOU HAVE PRODUCTS THAT APPEAL TO A WIDE RANGE OF TASTES AND POCKETBOOKS, YOU COULD DO WELL AT MALL SHOWS.

(c) Farmers' markets

Another variation on the traditional craft market is the selling of crafts at a farmers' market. These are now a regular feature in many towns and cities throughout the country. Many farmers' markets are similar in atmosphere to craft markets, with a lot of small vendors selling their own high-quality produce directly to the public. Some craftspeople sell their work regularly at farmers' markets and find them an excellent outlet.

3. How to get your work into shows

You should always try to book craft shows as far as possible in advance. Some of the best shows have waiting lists, so it may take some time before your work is accepted. But don't despair if a show's promoter tells you that your name is on a waiting list. Many promoters try to balance their shows with a certain proportion of potters, woodworkers, weavers, and other types of craftspeople. Your chances of getting into a show may depend on the category you are in.

In the meantime, if you are having difficulty because the shows you want to enter are full, try one of the mall shows. These are usually much easier to get into. But pick one of the better-class mall shows where there is good-quality merchandise and a high proportion of genuine craftspeople.

Most show promoters have a fairly straightforward application procedure. They will send you an application form and in most cases will require samples or slides of your work if you are a first-time exhibitor at their show. If your products are compact and easily transportable and actual samples are acceptable, this may be the best way to present your work. However, photos or slides are much easier to handle and send through the mail, and very often it is photos or slides that are required for jurying.

The most important thing to know about photos and slides of your work is that they are best made by a professional photographer. It is equally important that you inform the photographer exactly what you want. You do not want trick shots or pictures with fancy props that show off the photographer's skill. What you need are pictures of your work that show as clearly as possible and as close up as possible the kinds of techniques used and the material used in your products. Anything else is a waste of time and money.

Use a plastic or cardboard slide holder for your slides so that they can be handled without being smudged. Label each slide carefully. Write a concise description of the item and its actual size on the label. Remember to include adequate postage for the return of your slides when you send off your application.

Be sure to find out about the availability of electricity at a show. Most indoor shows supply electricity to boothholders, and this is usually indicated on the application. If you don't need electricity for demonstrating your work, you will definitely need it for lighting. The importance of lighting is dealt with below, but it is worth mentioning here as well because it is so critical to a successful craft show.

If you have specific location requirements, such as a corner booth or an outer wall, request these things in your application. Some show applications have a place on the form for this, with first-, second- and third-choice possibilities; others have an "additional requirements" space on their applications. It is not always possible for a promoter to handle all special requests, but most will do their best to accommodate you if you apply early enough.

Sometimes it is possible to pick your location. If the exhibit hall is roughly rectangular in shape you won't have to worry about avoiding out-of-the-way nooks and crannies. Corner booths are generally sought after because they are open to the public on two sides and offer more selling space. It is usually best to avoid locations that are too close to the main entrance, exits, the food area, or washrooms. These areas all attract a relatively heavy flow of traffic but it is usually through traffic, not browsing customers.

In filling out your application for a show, you can increase your chances of acceptance by mentioning any relevant experience you have had or awards you have won for your work or other shows in which you exhibit. If you are just starting out, you won't have a track record but you might make your application stand out from the rest of the crowd by writing a good, brief description of your work. Many application forms have a space for comments to the jury. You can use this or any other blank space on the form to bring out the strong points of your work. Say you make porcelain figurines, for example, and your work has a particularly interesting finish. You might way to say that you "...use original painting techniques in combination with traditional Aztec designs to produce a unique and luminous finish that makes almost everyone stop to look at these highly unusual figurines...." Be as pointed and succinct as you can but don't hold back

in describing the merits of your work. If you have a good product that you think will attract attention, let the promoters know. They are always on the lookout for fresh new ideas and products.

4. Preparing for craft shows

(a) Stock

Your preparation for a show should begin as far as possible in advance. You should plan carefully to have an adequate supply of stock on hand before the show. If you are entering a new show or you are just starting out in your craft business, you won't know how much you can expect to sell. You will have to go by information you have gleaned about the show beforehand from average reported booth sales and information from other craftspeople. The size of the town where the show is being held, the time of year, and the state of the local economy are other factors you can use to help you make an estimate of sales.

For shows in your home town, you can fetch extra stock from home if you need it. For most out-of-town shows, it is usually necessary to bring all your backup stock with you. If you sell out during a show, you will certainly know you need more stock the next time around!

(b) Storage and transport of stock

You will also need bags or boxes for transporting your goods to the show and storing your backup stock. Plastic garbage bags work fine for some kinds of soft goods where wrinkling isn't a problem. Pottery and many other types of products require something more substantial, such as cardboard or wooden boxes.

(c) Sales literature

Bring along plenty of sales literature when you go to a show, including an adequate supply of business cards and/or brochures that you hand out to anyone who seems like a prospective customer.

(d) Cash handling

You will need a receipt book to record your sales and sales tax collected. Bring plenty of change and some kind of cash box for carrying it in. To minimize the risk of theft, it is a good idea to use a nondescript box for carrying cash. Some craftspeople prefer an old tool box or even a cookie tin fitted out with divisions for the various coins and bills. Others carry their change in a leather purse strapped to their waist. In any case, it is a good idea to transfer larger bills from the cash box to some secure place on your person as quickly as possible.

(e) Packaging

It is essential to have an adequate supply of material to wrap your product in when you make a sale. Even if your goods are packaged, you should wrap them for the customer or drop them into a bag. Some craftspeople have bags printed with their company names and logos. When you are starting out you will want to keep your costs as low as possible, so you probably won't go in for anything as fancy as this. You can use paper bags or plastic shopping bags or knockdown cardboard boxes, depending on your product.

(f) Lighting

It is impossible to overemphasize the importance of lighting at a craft show. Simply put, the more light the better. Whether you use spot or flood lighting, your aim is to make your products stand out as much as possible. With some products, such as wooden toys, this is best accomplished by direct lighting; with others, such as many jewelry items, indirect lighting works better. Experiment until you get the best combination of light and shadow for your work. Bring at least one long heavy-duty extension cord and several shorter cords. The long cord is usually necessary to get power into your booth; the shorter ones distribute it to the various lighting fixtures. Use a multi-outlet breaker box to connect up the shorter cords to your long extension.

(g) Booth

Needless to say, your booth setup should be planned well in advance of the show. If you are doing shows for the first time, it is a good idea to set up your booth at home in your workshop or outside on the lawn to make sure everything will work out as planned and the booth will look the way you want it to.

Your aim in designing a booth is to create the most appropriate selling environment for your products. Since the type of booth fixtures you will use depends on the kinds of things you are selling, it is

hard to generalize about booth design. However, there are a couple of guiding principles that are worth remembering no matter what kind of product you make.

A display booth must not only set off your products in an attractive way, it should also be capable of being set up and taken down with relative ease. It should be light and compact enough to be easily transportable. As well — and this is a fact sometimes overlooked by beginners — a display setup must be flexible, that is, it must be capable of fitting into different-size booth spaces.

Most towns and cities have stores that specialize in the sale of display fixtures. Many cities also have companies that sell or rent fixtures for trade shows and exhibitions. You can often get ideas for your booth by visiting one of these stores or looking through their brochures.

One of the best places to look for booth ideas is a good craft market. Here you will see original and sometimes quite ingenious booth designs. In planning your booth, the sky is the limit and, if you want to, you can design and build your own unique booth from the ground up. However, in the beginning, while you are still in the process of getting your feet wet and both budget and time are strictly limited, you may want to adopt the simplest possible setup.

One of the simplest and most versatile setups — and for some craftspeople, still one of the best — is an arrangement of covered display tables. Tables can be easily arranged in different configurations to fit different booth sizes and shapes. Another advantage is that they are sometimes provided by the show promoter or can be ordered as an extra, so you have one less thing to haul to the show. The display tables you get at shows are usually only one size, so it is a good idea to bring along one or two smaller tables of your own. This allows you to make L-shaped or U-shaped configurations that might not be possible if all the tables were of the same size.

Starting with a basic arrangement of tables, you can use a variety of simple options to increase the effectiveness of your display. You can increase the display area and raise the level of the display by the use of "add-ons" like backboards or risers. Backboards are simply pieces of plywood or pegboard, appropriately draped or painted, that you attach to the back of your table. Risers are tiered or stepped shelves that allow you to raise the level of your display and give you vertical as well as horizontal display space. They are available from display companies in cardboard, which easily knocks down for transport, or you can build your own out of wood. Another useful add-on for a basic table display is an arched sign that can be attached to a table. In addition to being a good place to affix a sign, this also gives you a high, solid structure to which you can attach a variety of floodlights, spotlights, or track-lighting fixtures.

The choice of table coverings is also important. Your coverings should be in solid colors rather than prints or patterns, which tend to distract the eye. You don't want anything in your booth that takes attention away from your products. The color should be chosen as far as possible to contrast with the predominant tones of the products in your display (i.e., darker coverings for light products, lighter shades for dark items). Generally speaking, it is best to use soft-textured fabrics like velour or velveteen for hard-surfaced items like wood products and jewelry, and hard-textured fabrics, such as cotton, polyester, or satin, for soft products like woven goods. However, there is no hard and fast rule here and your primary aim is to find the best backdrop for your products to make them stand out and to focus the customer's attention.

In planning your booth, you will need to think about places for your backup stock, packaging, receipt book, cash box, and calculator. These items should be easily accessible and yet be out of sight of the public. The underside of draped tables and risers are good places for storing your backup stock.

Plan your booth with a place in mind for you to sit or stand while you sell. It is highly impractical to work a booth from the aisle. You will need a chair but take note that most chairs are not high enough to permit you to see over the top of your display if you are sitting behind it. You should either buy a folding chair with extra long legs or extend the legs of an existing chair by short lengths of heavy-duty plastic piping.

If you have taken time and trouble to create an attractive display, you don't want the effect spoiled by having it next to the unfinished outer wall of your neighbor's booth. Therefore, you should include a backdrop as part of your booth setup. If it is possible to incorporate the backdrop as part of your display by using pegboard or light shelving, so much the better. For the basic table arrangement described above, the simplest backdrop is a curtain draped over a thin, lightweight frame. Or you can use a number of room dividers. Either way, you should make sure that the colors and finish of the backdrop complement the rest of your display.

IT IS ALWAYS EASIER

WHEN YOU HAVE HELP

AT A SHOW.

Positioning of the products in your booth can sometimes make a considerable difference to sales. Once again, there are no hard and fast rules. Generally speaking, it is best to arrange your products in such a way that the items to which you wish to draw the most attention are positioned as close as possible to eye level. Smaller items should be placed at the front; the larger, big-ticket items in the rear or just above eye level.

Mark prices clearly on everything for sale. Do not rely on signs saying "Widgets, $15.50 Lg., $8.95 Sm." Many customers are hesitant about looking more closely at an item if the price is not clearly displayed.

5. How to sell your work at shows

This is one of the easiest parts of all, since most quality, handcrafted items sell themselves. Well, almost. There are a few simple things you can do to help.

Start out by getting a good night's sleep before a show. If you are tired or grumpy, it will be hard to have a good show. Plan to arrive early at the exhibition hall or fairground, preferably the night before for out-of-town shows, and allow yourself plenty of time to set up your booth. Then have a short rest or a snack or take a stroll before the show opens to the public.

It is always easier when you have help at a show. A spouse, child, or obliging friend comes in handy at a show. Even if you prefer to do most of the actual selling yourself, it makes good sense to have someone there so you can take a break from time to time.

Be polite and attentive to your customers and don't read or talk to your neighbor in the next booth while there are customers around. On the other hand, don't hover over customers and make them feel uncomfortable. Try to look confident and relaxed and never appear too anxious to make a sale. Customers appreciate cheerful, attentive service, but many will be turned off if you try a hard-sell technique. If possible, engage a customer in casual conversation; it's surprisingly easy to do at a craft market and sometimes leads to very interesting conversations. But don't get carried away by good conversation; remember your purpose is to sell your products.

Most customers will signify their intention to purchase by asking you a question, by making eye contact, or picking up the item they are interested in. Usually, by this time, the decision to buy has already been made and all you have to do is take the customer's money. This is about as easy as it can get.

While not every customer question signals an intention to buy, it does give you an extra opportunity to make a sale. Often a customer will make a specific query about a product or ask a more general question like "Did you make these?" Don't launch into a prearranged sales pitch at this point. Just answer the question politely and let your own enthusiasm and confidence in your work find their natural expression. As a craftsperson, these are your "secret weapons" to help you sell. You made the product you are selling, you own the company, you are doing what you like, and you are good at it (and you are making all the profits!). You don't need to deliver hype; all you have to do is be yourself, relaxed and natural. This is the best sales pitch of all.

Normally this is all the sales technique you require at craft markets. Sometimes, however, especially in the sale of big-ticket items or custom work, some additional selling might be required. This is because decisions to purchase more expensive items or products requiring custom work and/or fitting usually require a bit of service from the salesperson.

There are certain tried and proven techniques that help you sell more expensive items. The best way of illustrating these is to give an example of one of the most successful craftspeople we know. Chantal's methods are so effective, she could be a textbook example of how to sell almost anything.

Chantal makes high-quality women's clothing. Most of her products cost $150 or more, yet they sell like hotcakes. There are quite a number of other craftspeople who sell competitively priced work of equal quality. Yet this woman consistently outsells her competitors year after year. How does she do it? Simply put, she does it because she knows how to sell.

First, she does not rely only on the walk-in traffic at a show. Before a show opens, Chantal contacts current and prospective customers by mail or telephone and invites them to visit her booth. She has a file containing the names and addresses of previous customers (from sales receipts) and from a guest book she maintains at every show where she gets the names of people who visit her booth.

Once a prospective customer has stepped inside her booth and has had a chance to look around, Chantal strikes up a conversation. This is not difficult to do and anyone can do it simply by following

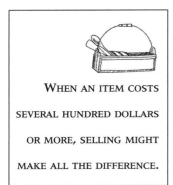

WHEN AN ITEM COSTS SEVERAL HUNDRED DOLLARS OR MORE, SELLING MIGHT MAKE ALL THE DIFFERENCE.

her method. If the customer is familiar to her from a previous sale, he or she is welcomed back. If the prospective customer is new, Chantal begins by offering useful and helpful information about her products. This is usually sufficient to get the customer into a conversation from which Chantal can determine if he or she is likely to make a purchase.

Chantal does not begin her sales pitch or presentation by simply reciting a description of her product line. Instead, she concentrates on the particular items in which the customer has expressed interest. For example, a customer may have looked at or picked up a blue sweater and matching scarf. Or the customer may be looking for advice on something that will go with her particular coloring and hair style.

Chantal always aims at getting her female customers to try on her clothes. Once that happens, "I almost always get a sale," she says. To clinch the matter at that point, she will deal with any objections the customer may have. Is the item too big, too small, the wrong color? In each case Chantal is ready with answers. "I have the same style in red," she will say. Or "would you like the blue to be a little lighter?" She praises the effect of a product on a customer's appearance: "That suits you very well, don't you think?" And she does all this in such a way that her customers never feel she is "pushy" or too aggressive.

By this time, the customer feels that she will look good in Chantal's clothing. If the customer is a male, he is convinced that his wife, girlfriend, or daughter will look good in it. (Chantal's sales methods seem to work equally well with both men and women, though the majority of her customers are women.) The customer also feels at this point that Chantal's work is good value for the money and that he or she is being given first-class service. Now, very little is needed to close the sale.

If there is still hesitation or further objections, Chantal is ready with an appropriate response. If a customer hesitates over the price, perhaps feeling that the item in question is too expensive, Chantal will lay stress on the high quality of the materials and the detailed work involved. Or if a customer suggests that he or she will "come back later," Chantal will often point out that this is inadvisable because she has a limited number of the item in question and she wouldn't want the customer to be disappointed. She means this, too — it's not just sales hype. Her products sell so well that customers who walk away to "think about it" do take a chance on missing out.

Of course most handcrafted products will not require this kind of selling, but when an item costs several hundred dollars or more, selling might make all the difference. For Chantal it certainly does. She outsells her competitors year after year, not because her products or prices are better than theirs, but because she knows how to make the sale.

c. Retailing Your Work through the Mail

For some craftworkers, mail order has been a profitable way of selling their work. In North America, billions of dollars worth of products are sold through the mail every year. Most of the material now placed in mailboxes is advertising. Mail order is essentially a marketing method in which you bring your product to the attention of the customer who then places an order by mail. You can solicit mail orders by placing advertisements in the media or by mailing advertising material directly to potential customers.

1. Direct mail

In *bulk mailings*, material is sent to all the householders in a given geographic area. In *direct mail* solicitation, material is sent to individuals on a particular mailing list.

Because it is addressed individually, direct mail generally commands more attention than bulk mail. It is also possible to target specific groups through a direct mailing. You can use a mailing list that you have compiled yourself, comprised of customers who have visited your booth in the past year or who have previously ordered from you. Or you can purchase or rent mailing lists from companies that specialize in mail-order solicitation. Such lists are available for just about any imaginable group in the country on the basis of age, sex, ethnicity, profession, residence, buying habits, and so on.

A *compiled* list is a list of people who share a common characteristic. For instance, they may all be members of a certain association or a certain profession — a list of dentists, for example. This one characteristic is all you know about these people. They may or may not be direct-mail purchasers.

Respondent lists, on the other hand, are drawn up on the basis of responses to previous direct-mail solicitation by other companies. Respondent lists may indicate that the addressees are more likely to purchase a particular product through the mail. Compiled lists cost around $30 to $50 per thousand; respondent lists cost around $100 per thousand.

Direct-mail solicitation is expensive. In addition to the mailing list and postage, there is the cost of brochures and stationery and the time involved in organizing the mailing. At the very least, each item mailed will cost about 60¢ in the U.S. and 70¢ or more in Canada, depending on the cost of the advertising material you are sending out. Since a response rate of 3 percent is considered good, your cost per contact could be in the range of approximately $15 to $25. Needless to say, you must have a product with a very good profit margin to afford this kind of advertising. It is also important to remember that the costs of mail order are all "up-front"; that is, they require you to lay out substantial amounts of money (on brochures, mailing lists, postage, etc.) before you get anything in return.

Certain mail-order solicitation techniques are much more effective than others, and unless you have an effective method, you won't even achieve the 3 percent rate. Much depends on how you design your brochures or other advertising materials. Even the envelope you use is important. Some mail-order firms don't wait for a prospective customer to open their envelopes. They know that a lot of advertising mail is simply thrown away on sight, so they employ highly paid graphic artists to design eye-catching logos and messages that they print on the outside of their envelopes. These are designed to catch a prospective customer's attention and induce him or her to open and read the material inside.

There are numerous other tricks of the mail-order trade that are beyond the scope of this book. If you are interested in additional information, you should contact the National Mail Order Association or visit their Web site:

National Mail Order Association
2807 Polk St. NE Minneapolis MN 55418-2954
Tel: 612-788-1673 Fax: 612-788-1147
www.nmoa.org
E-mail: info@nmoa.org

For the average small craft business, direct mail will not be a very feasible option, except perhaps on the basis of a list compiled from the craftsperson's own customers. Every customer who visits your booth, whether they buy anything or not, should receive one of your brochures or product information sheets and be encouraged to sign your "guest book." That way there is the possibility that they may become customers at some future date. Of course, your purpose in attending a craft show is to sell your products on the spot, not at some vague time in the future. Still, there are always customers who would purchase your product at a later date if they could order it through the mail. This spinoff kind of mail-order marketing can be a fairly lucrative adjunct to your craft-market sales.

2. Advertising to solicit mail orders

Advertising in large daily newspapers will generally not be of much value to craftspeople. While these newspapers reach vast numbers of people, they are not usually kept longer than a day and they are rarely read from beginning to end. Small advertisements have little chance of being noticed alongside the advertisements of corporations with big advertising budgets.

Magazine advertisements can be useful for generating mail-order business. Besides having a much longer life than newspapers, magazines are more likely to be read from cover to cover by more than one person. Magazines are also targeted toward specific groups (e.g., gardeners, career women, etc.) so you can be sure of reaching a group that is likely to buy your products. Also, many magazines have mail-order sections and their subscribers are used to ordering products by mail.

Apart from small classified ads, advertising in a national or general-interest magazine is very expensive. A full-page ad in a national magazine can cost $20,000 or more. There are, however, a lot of specialty magazines with classified sections where ads can be placed for $200 or even less. Trade magazines and travel magazines (such as those put out by the airlines) are frequently less expensive than other types of magazines for small classified advertisements.

Chapter 6

WHOLESALING YOUR WORK

a. What Kinds of Shops Can You Sell To?

Selling work to stores is probably one of the most effective marketing methods for the full-time production craftworker. By selling your work to stores, you can greatly increase the size of your market. Letting stores handle sales to the consumer allows you to concentrate your own time and energy on production and design.

You must be careful to select the best retail outlets for your work. It will help if we divide possible retail craft outlets into six categories:

(i) Galleries

(ii) Craft shops

(iii) Gift/craft shops

(iv) Gift shops

(v) Department stores

(vi) Other stores

While not every shop will fall neatly into one of these categories,

you will find the classification helpful in deciding where to direct your marketing efforts.

1. Galleries

A gallery will usually be interested in one-of-a-kind pieces rather than production crafts. Selling your work through a gallery can bring a lot of prestige but, in most cases, won't bring you much money on a regular basis unless you have an established reputation in your medium. Galleries are usually interested in work where the value and profit margin are relatively high. A gallery's commission can range up to 50 percent of the selling price. Moreover, most galleries only accept work on a consignment basis, paying you if and when your work is sold.

CRAFT SHOPS ARE THE BEST OUTLET FOR THE PRODUCTION CRAFTWORKER.

2. Craft shops

This type of shop specializes in the sale of high-quality, handmade work. It is the best outlet for the production craftworker. Consider only craft shops that are in high-volume traffic locations and that carry work compatible with your own. Look for stores that carry only high-quality work; avoid those that sell cheap "craftsy" items and mass-produced novelties.

There are a few large retail craft enterprises with several branches, but most craft stores are small, owner-managed operations, usually run by people with previous experience in the craft field. Some shops are run by craftspeople as an adjunct to their workshop. There are craft shops that specialize in a particular medium (e.g., fabric arts, pottery). Others are restricted to work of a specific region (e.g., a particular state or province) or a particular theme (e.g., early pioneer). But most shops carry a fairly broad cross section of handcrafted work.

3. Gift/craft shops

A gift/craft shop does not usually advertise itself as such, but it is essentially a gift shop that specializes in exclusive, high-quality, mass-produced giftware as well as handcrafted products. Giftware covers such a broad range of products that it is almost impossible to define. What is important in looking at the gift/craft shop is the overall quality

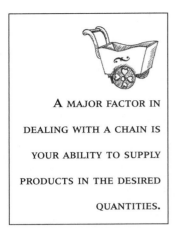

A MAJOR FACTOR IN
DEALING WITH A CHAIN IS
YOUR ABILITY TO SUPPLY
PRODUCTS IN THE DESIRED
QUANTITIES.

of the merchandise sold and the reputation of the shop, as well as its location.

Some gift/craft shops have been in business for generations and their names are synonymous with high-quality goods. Many of these products are handcrafted, though their main selling point is not so much that they are handmade as the fact that their brands or trade names are highly respected and sought after for quality or uniqueness (e.g., certain types of English and European porcelain).

For the large-scale production craft business, the gift/craft shop will be an important outlet. It can frequently sell a higher volume of merchandise than the craft shop. If they carry well-known and popular lines of giftware, gift/craft shops will often be able to afford the big overhead costs associated with locations in high-traffic areas like airports, train stations, and big downtown shopping malls. (Note: shops in places like airports and train stations will sometimes mark up your products by as much as 150 percent.)

A number of large, high-quality gift chains fit into the gift/craft category. These can offer you a regional or even national market. Although their purchasing is not always centralized, a product that is successful in one store has an excellent chance of being sold in other stores in the chain.

For years, a friend of mine had been trying to interest one of the major chains in his leatherwork. Though his work was selling well in craft shops, the chain's head buyer remained unconvinced. One of the chain's stores happened to be located not far from his studio. By dint of sheer persistence and some free samples, my friend persuaded the local store manager to try a small order of his products. They sold very quickly and within a few weeks he got a call from the chain's head buyer. Within a year, my friend's work was being sold by more than a dozen stores in the chain.

A major factor in dealing with a chain is your ability to supply products in the desired quantities, of consistent quality, and on time. These requirements are important in the service you provide to all your customers, but the difference in dealing with a chain is that it is likely to require much larger quantities. You must be certain that you can produce the required quantities before you take large orders from a chain. It takes time to increase your output. (See chapters 15 and 16 on expanding your business.)

4. Gift shops

Many of the shops that advertise themselves as gift shops are characterized chiefly by the great variety of low-quality, cheap, mass-produced products they sell. These shops are not usually good outlets for hand-crafted items.

Occasionally, a gift shop will have a separate section displaying handmade products. Such a shop might be worth considering as an outlet for your work if there is a high volume of business in the area (e.g., if the area is a major tourist attraction) and no better-quality shop to which you can sell. You must think of your professional reputation. If your work appears in a cheap or junky shop, it may be harder to sell to some of the better-quality gift/craft and craft shops.

5. Department stores

In the mid-seventies, a few New York stores, such as Saks Fifth Avenue, began selling craft items in a limited way. Now, department stores throughout the United States and Canada are handling hand-crafted items. Some have specialized craft departments, but hand-crafted items can be found in a variety of other departments, including gift, jewelry, and housewares.

Department store sales should be considered in the light of their possible effects on your other customers. If you get a large department-store order, it may pre-empt an entire season's production. Great, you don't need to worry about finding other customers. But what if the next time around you do not get the large department-store order?

Some of your small customers may be reluctant to do business with you if you are selling to a large department store in the same area. It is safer not to put all your eggs in one basket. While it's nice to have some large accounts, it's not healthy if any one of them has too high a proportion of your total sales. If more than 15 percent or 20 percent of your business is with a single account, you are probably relying too much on that one customer. Your overall sales and profit situation could be seriously harmed if you fail to secure a big repeat order.

6. Other stores

Outlets for crafts aren't restricted to the above five types. We have sold our toys to a men's dress shop (as props), museum gift shops, and even banks. The list of possible outlets for crafts includes plant,

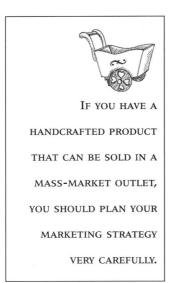

furniture, dress, and sewing shops. Indeed, with a little imagination, you can sell your products to just about any kind of shop where quality merchandise is sold. The first five categories are the most promising places to start. But don't limit yourself to any particular type of shop.

b. Mass-Market Outlets

Be careful of the "perils of success." Let's say that your marketing efforts are starting to pay off, and you have placed your products in a variety of craft and gift shops. You are so successful, in fact, that retailers are beginning to approach you with inquiries about your products.

The best retailers are always on the lookout for new merchandise. Sometimes handcrafted products are sought by marketers for "superstores" or stores selling "high-tech" merchandise. Should you consider selling your work in such a marketplace?

I know at least one producer of handcrafted leather goods who has developed a good market with a major national brand manufacturer. This craftsperson makes customized leather cases for electronic products such as portable radios, cellular telephones, and laptop computers. Her products are sold in "big box" superstores amidst an array of computer and office merchandise.

If you have a handcrafted product that can be sold in such a mass-market outlet, you should plan your marketing strategy very carefully. You will first have to be certain that you have the productive capacity to handle such sales.

There are certain risks with mass-market sales. As with department store sales, you may end up with too high a proportion of your total sales to one or two big customers. Also, the presence of your products in mass-market outlets may make it difficult to sell your work to craft and gift shops.

You can avoid some of these pitfalls by developing different product lines. You can have a one-of-a-kind or designer product line for craft shops and galleries and a production line for gift and department stores.

A lot depends on the products you are making, the quantities you are capable of producing, and the kind of craft business you wish to have. If your business is a small, one-person operation, as is the case with most craft businesses, you will probably not need or want to expand your sales beyond galleries, craft shops, and gift shops. But if you plan to enlarge your business, perhaps hiring other people to work for you, you may wish to explore sales opportunities beyond the traditional craft outlets. (See chapters 15 and 16 on expanding your craft business and hiring others to work for you.)

c. How to Get Your Products into Shops

1. Calling on stores

At an early stage in your business career, visit those stores in your own area that would appear to be good outlets for your work. Where you start depends largely on the kind of product you have. For one-of-a-kind items, try galleries and craft shops. For production crafts, you might try any of the different types listed above, bearing in mind that the craft shop and the gift/craft shop are probably the best places to start.

When you call on stores, make certain that you talk to the person with purchasing authority. In most cases, this will be the store owner or manager. With chains or department-store buyers, an appointment in advance is mandatory. Indeed, it's a good idea to arrange an appointment with any store buyer. Most of these people are extremely busy and your chances of success are much higher if you approach them when they are free to listen to you.

When you meet a store buyer, be as relaxed as possible and confident about your work. When you make your sales pitch, don't be inhibited about praising your own work. If you have a lot of faith in your product, let the buyer know it. You should bring actual samples of your work; don't rely on brochures or photographs. If you have already established a clientele for your work through craft markets or your own retail store, point this out to the buyer. Listen attentively to what the buyer has to say about your product and be prepared to answer any questions.

If you don't get an answer one way or the other during the first visit, be sure to leave a brochure, price list, and business card to remind the buyer of your call. If the store does most of its purchasing during a certain period of the year, be sure to call or visit again at that time.

2. The trade show

Once you are successful in placing your products in stores in your immediate area, you may want to extend your marketing efforts further

afield. If you enjoy travel and like meeting people, you might want to make extended sales trips to promote your products. Chances are, however, that the demands of production will make it impossible for you to be on the road for long periods if your business is growing. You will need some other way to reach those out-of-town customers. One way of doing this is to exhibit your products at a wholesale trade show.

There are many similarities between trade shows and retail/craft shows, so much of the information given in chapter 5 on exhibiting at craft shows applies equally well to trade shows.

Unlike retail shows, the wholesale or trade show is not open to the public but only to store owners who place orders for future delivery. There are now several dozen wholesale craft shows in North America and many more gift shows where handcrafted products are sold. (For information on finding wholesale shows, see Appendix 1.) A wholesale show usually involves more planning than a retail show but, unlike the retail show, a wholesale show does not require that you bring a lot of stock with you. Booth fees are usually much higher than for retail shows. In the case of out-of-town shows, there are travel and accommodation costs as well.

You should draw up a budget for a wholesale show. Make a list of all the expenses you expect to incur and arrive at an estimate of your total costs. Estimate as realistically as possible how much business you expect the show to generate. This can be difficult the first time around, but you should at least know the amount of sales you have to achieve in order to cover your costs. In estimating your costs, don't forget to include your own time while actually selling at the show.

Before exhibiting at a show, it is a good idea to visit the show first as a spectator and do a reconnaissance. Most trade shows are closed to the general public, but you can gain admission as a buyer simply by using your business card or company letterhead. There is a wealth of information to be gained by visiting a show beforehand, looking at the kinds of products for sale, and comparing prices and quality with your own. If you visit a show as a spectator, remember that most of the people there are intent on doing business. Be discreet and don't get in the way.

When planning for a trade show, design your display so that your booth looks full without appearing overcrowded. Choose the type of display unit that complements your products. Some of the most beautiful displays I have seen were designed and built by craftworkers especially for their own products.

Dress conservatively and neatly. Remember, these are business professionals that you are trying to impress. Be alert and attentive and ready to help the customer at all times. Don't appear bored, and don't read a book in the booth. Some customers will want to browse the booth in a leisurely fashion. Others will want you to conduct them around, describing the products as you go and providing them with any necessary information.

Try to feel out how much attention the buyer wants and give it to him or her. Learn to distinguish between the lookers and the buyers at a show. Be polite to lookers, but don't waste too much time on them. Concentrate on the buyers.

Your basic approach to selling should be the same as in craft shows. There is a significant difference, however, in a wholesale show: your customers are not consumers but business people who want to make money for themselves or their employers by selling your products in their stores. Accordingly, it is your job as a salesperson to convince them not only that your work is good, but also that it sells and that you will provide them with good service. Making a sale at a trade show means getting an order, and the technique is similar to that needed to sell big-ticket items at a craft show. (See chapter 5.)

When you get that order, don't forget to have it signed and get the purchase order number if there is one. Don't be embarrassed to ask for the buyer's signature. It is standard business practice. Have your terms of sale, delivery time, and minimum order printed clearly on the order form. When you take the order, ask for credit references. If you are selling to someone for the first time, make certain that you check out their credit worthiness before shipping goods to them. (See the section on granting credit in chapter 14.)

3. The sales representative

Another way to reach out-of-town customers is to use the services of a sales representative or sales agent. This is someone who will take your samples and literature around to shops and obtain orders for you. He or she is usually paid on a commission basis (a certain percentage of the value of the orders taken).

A good sales representative, or rep, is one of the best ways of reaching new out-of-town customers and following up on those accounts that you opened at the trade show. Picking the right rep is not easy. In fact, the selection of a sales rep is one of the most difficult

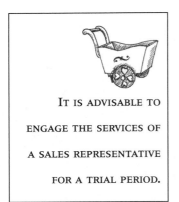

problems the small craft business faces. Many craft businesses have had unfortunate experiences with sales reps, frequently because they were not sufficiently selective in their choices.

What should you look for in a rep? You want someone who has an understanding and appreciation of handcrafted work and experience in selling to craft and gift/craft shops. There are very few reps who restrict themselves entirely to handcrafted products; most carry gift lines as well. This in itself should be no problem, provided the giftware lines are compatible with your products in quality and price.

One of the most important things to know about a rep is the number and kind of lines he or she is carrying. It does no good to engage a rep who is carrying 30 or 40 other lines. There is simply no way your product can get the attention it deserves from a rep who has so many different products. Find out what size territory the rep is covering. If it's too big, the rep won't be able to properly cover it. Conversely, too small a territory raises the danger that the rep will work it too intensively for a handcrafted product like yours. (See chapter 8 for some of the dangers of overselling your work.)

How do you go about locating a rep? If you have already started to market your work, you may be approached by salespeople who have seen some of your things in stores and craft markets and are interested in representing you. Perhaps a fellow craftworker can recommend a rep. An ad placed in the classified section of the newspaper can sometimes help, though these tend to attract unlikely prospects, such as people with no sales experience. It is better to place your ad in a trade publication where it is more likely to be seen by experienced salespeople. Some trade shows have a notice board where you can put an advertisement for a sales representative.

Sales representatives often advertise in the various specialty trade magazines, or they can be located by referring to directories of sales reps such as those listed in Appendix 1.

It is advisable to engage the services of a sales representative for a trial period of, say, six months. This should be long enough in most cases to reveal the kind of results you can expect to get from this rep. A good rep should be able to get your work into stores where he or she has already established connections and is selling other lines. If the rep can't do this much, you have probably picked the wrong person.

Most sales representatives will expect exclusivity within the territory assigned to them. This means that the salesperson is entitled to a commission on all sales within the defined territory. It is usually possible to have a limited number of house accounts, which you have opened yourself and on which you do not have to pay the salesperson any commission. Otherwise, he or she has the territory tied up for the duration of the sales agreement. This is a powerful reason for keeping your initial trial period as short as possible.

Rates of commission for people in the gift/craft business vary, but you can expect to pay anywhere from 10 percent to 20 percent; 15 percent is about the norm. You would pay less to a rep in a territory that you had already substantially opened up, and you would probably have to pay more to a sales agency with a showroom in a major urban location and a force of salespeople on the road.

It is a good idea to offer your rep some kind of incentive plan where the rate of commission escalates on sales over a certain level. Make sure that you have a clear understanding with the rep about when sales commissions are payable. If your customer terms are net 30 days, you will have to wait at least a month for your money. You should pay your salespeople commissions for the month's sales at the end of the following month. You must also retain control over the granting of credit and ship only those orders that meet your credit requirements.

When you sell your work through a sales rep, you must, above all, be sure that the person who represents you appreciates and believes in your work. Someone who is half-hearted about your products cannot sell them properly. Your sales representative should have some general knowledge of your production techniques so that he or she can explain your work to customers. Your rep should also know your production capabilities, and you should have a mutual understanding about how much business you expect his or her efforts to generate.

4.   The wholesale distributor

Many products are sold through wholesalers or distributors who purchase relatively large quantities of goods outright and sell them to retailers in a given territory. An arrangement of this kind can rid you of all marketing problems and enable you to concentrate entirely on production. You are also free of much of the paperwork associated with invoicing, billing, and accounts receivable.

There are, however, very few established distributors or wholesalers of handcrafted products in the United States and Canada. One of the main reasons is that most handcrafted products are not able to bear the usual wholesaler markup. This markup can be from 25 percent to 50 percent and more, with the retailer's markup on top of that.

A distributor's markup of, say, 40 percent would mean that an item you sold to the distributor for $10 would be sold by the distributor to the retailer for $14. Since most retailers mark up by 100 percent, the item would retail for $28 in the store. With sales tax added on (in many jurisdictions), the final price to the customer is likely to be $30 — three times the price you got for the item! Needless to say, there are not many handcrafted items that can sell very briskly when they are marked up this much.

5. Wholesaling your work on the Internet

The next chapter in this book deals with retailing your work on the Internet. When most people think of selling crafts online, it is retail that they think of. But the Net can also be used to market your work to shops and galleries. If you are already well-versed in retailing your crafts online, you may want to go directly to section 1 of Chapter 7, which deals with online wholesaling. If you have little or no experience in Internet sales, you should read Chapter 7 from the beginning.

Chapter 7
SELLING YOUR WORK ONLINE

The Internet offers new and exciting possibilities for crafts. More and more craftspeople are using the Net as a marketing tool, a way of tracking down new suppliers, finding out about craft markets, and keeping in touch with one another. Some craftspeople are selling their products online, either on their own Web sites or on one of the many online stores specializing in crafts.

Should you sell your crafts online? How do you go about getting your work on the Internet? This chapter will help you answer these questions. But before looking at specific ways of selling your work online, it is useful to look briefly at some of the basic aspects of the Internet itself. An understanding of the nature of the Net is the essential first step in developing a strategy to put your work online.

a. The Basics

The Internet is one of the main driving forces behind what some people call the new economy or the world of e-commerce — the exchange of business information using such processes as electronic data interchange, e-mail, and electronic funds transfer. Many call these technologies revolutionary. Setting aside the hype that frequently accompanies new technologies, there is no doubt that the

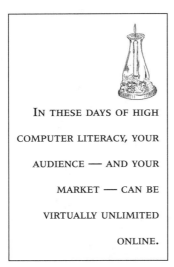

Internet has led to major changes in the way individuals and companies do business.

Accurate statistics of the numbers of people online are difficult to give because Internet use is growing so rapidly. E-commerce is also growing at a tremendous rate. In 1997, 24 percent of U.S. businesses had access to the Internet; by 2001, this number had increased to an estimated 45 percent. The percentage of households in North America that are connected to the Internet is even larger, and growing at least as rapidly.

The Internet can be accessed from anywhere in the world, provided that you have a computer (or computer-like device) and an Internet connection. In these days of high computer literacy, your audience — and your market — can be virtually unlimited online. New wireless technologies allow the transmission of digital signals between computers without physical connections — potential buyers could be as close as their cell phones. Almost every computer available has hardware and software already installed that will allow you to connect to the Internet. Most telephone and cable companies can provide you with Internet service. The ubiquitous and ever-growing presence of the Internet makes it a sales tool your business cannot afford to ignore.

Web browsers and automated search engines make the Internet extremely user-friendly, even for the technically challenged among us. Ease of use is just one of the reasons why the Web is so popular. Its other fundamental features include its global reach and the fact that it is interactive, allowing users to input as well as receive information. In terms of e-commerce, these features make it possible for a dialogue between buyers and sellers anywhere in the world.

You don't need your own Web site — or even your own computer — to put your business on the Internet. Web developers can create and maintain a Web site for you, either as a separate site under your company name or as part of a crafts site or Internet mall featuring work by a variety of craftspeople. All you have to do is send in pictures of your work along with descriptive text and graphics. The Web developer does the rest, including scanning in your pictures and arranging your text and any graphics you may require.

If you choose this option, you don't have to concern yourself with the issues involved in building and maintaining your own Web site, let alone registering and hosting your site. Registering your site with search engines is necessary to enable prospective customers to find your company on the Internet. Hosting refers to the actual location of your site. Web sites are not virtual places; they reside on actual computers in real locations. These computers, together with the powerful software needed to run them, are referred to as servers. Whether you have a developer build and maintain your site or you build your own site, you will need to have your site hosted on a server. It does not matter where your site is hosted physically, because software is available that allows you to set up and maintain your Web site remotely.

Which option is best: your own site, or someone else's, or an Internet mall specializing in crafts? And if you decide to have your own site, should you build it yourself, use one of the "ready-to-go" electronic storefronts available on the Net, or should you hire someone to build your own unique site? How do you go about finding and hiring a Web-site developer? What about marketing your site and making your online venture profitable? Each of these questions is answered in detail below.

b. Can You Sell Your Crafts Online?

As I said at the beginning of this book, the popularity of fine handcrafted products is due in part to a reaction against our high-tech society and its cheap mass-market products. As such, handcrafted items might, at first glance, seem to be unlikely products to be bought and sold on the Internet. Furthermore, one of the most important venues in which handcrafted items have been traditionally sold, the craft show or fair, is in some ways almost the exact opposite of the Internet.

A good craft show is always something of an event for both vendors and sellers, and the atmosphere at the best shows is colorful and even festive. The sights, sounds, and smells of the market, the bustle of the crowd — all these contribute to an ambiance that can only be found in such a setting. It is a tactile experience too; you can run your hand over the surface of oiled wood or fine-tooled leather. There is also a social dimension to a craft market — you can meet friends there and you can speak with the person who actually makes the product.

There is no way a Web site can simulate, let alone recreate, this kind of experience. Even the best craft shops and galleries cannot do this. Nor do they need to; obviously, handcrafted products sell in places other than craft shows. There are many potential purchasers who have neither the time nor the inclination to visit shows, just as there are purchasers who wish to buy during times when, and in

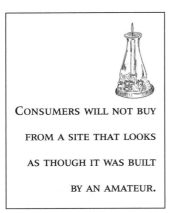

places where, there simply are no crafts shows. For customers like these, the Web offers the advantages of convenience and speed. Surveys show that saving time is the reason most often given by Internet users for shopping online.

An online store is open twenty-four hours a day, seven days a week. There is no waiting in line and no need to worry about traffic tie-ups to get there. And there is another important feature of the Web that is extremely useful to a craft business: the Web is highly visual, capable of showing detailed photographs and sophisticated graphics. Research into Web-based marketing has shown that products such as artwork, crafts, and gifts can be sold on the Web if they are presented properly, making full use of the Internet's graphic capabilities.

The importance of presentation for artwork and crafts cannot be overestimated. To make this even clearer, contrast artwork and crafts with what Web marketers call commodity products. For commodity products, presentation is less important — you know what a book or a compact disc looks like. What matters to you as a potential buyer of commodity products is not so much the actual appearance of the item but the price, selection, and availability. Commodity products are generally, though not necessarily, easier than most other kinds of products to sell on the Web.

With artwork and crafts, the appearance and the quality of the product are paramount. Therefore, proper presentation of the product is critical if it is to be successfully marketed on the Web. Consumers will not buy from a site that looks as though it was built by an amateur.

Poorly designed and badly built Web sites are all too common. Because putting together a Web site is becoming technically easier every year and has now reached a point where virtually anyone with a modicum of computer skill can build one, too many people are tempted to try. The results show up on the Web all the time. Some Web sites are not just boring — some actually detract from the product or message they are trying to promote.

Most craftspeople would not bring their products to a craft fair, plunk them down on a bare tabletop, and expect the public to buy. As discussed in Chapter 5, the most successful craftspeople take pains to present their work in the most attractive setting possible, and many of them show great ingenuity in devising unique and interesting displays for their products.

Presenting your product on the Internet is not all that different. Unless you have a handcrafted product that is so well-known that it can be sold like a commodity — and no craftsperson ever does — you need to give the same amount of care and attention to your Web presentation as you do to your display booth in a craft fair. Whether you put your products into someone else's online store or you build your own, a good presentation is critical to your success.

c. Online Craft Stores — Finding the Best Ones

Selling your work in someone else's online craft store is by far the simplest and least expensive way to get your products on the Net. If you decide to sell through one of the online stores specializing in crafts, you will save yourself the time, effort, and expense of building and promoting your own Web site. There is much to be said for going this route. If you are new to the Internet, not comfortable with computers, or heavily involved with the production side of your business, it makes good sense to leave online sales to someone else.

There are hundreds of online stores where you could possibly sell crafts but, with some exceptions, you are likely to get better results (i.e., higher sales) if you concentrate your efforts on stores specializing in artwork or crafts. This is because of the way we look for things to buy on the Net. Surveys show that most people start out with a search for a specific type of product or service.

In the section on marketing (see Chapter 6), we saw that crafts can be sold in other kinds of shops besides craft shops. Gift stores and even department stores have successfully sold craft items. Similarly, on the Net it is possible to sell your handmade place mats in an online store specializing in tableware, for example, or your handmade bracelets in an online jewelry store. Some craftspeople have done well in online stores with a narrow focus, but most who try this approach find themselves competing against factory-made products.

By and large, your chances of success are greater in an online store that specializes in crafts. That said, it is worth noting that marketing on the Net is evolving very rapidly; new stores are coming online all the time and innovative marketing opportunities are constantly emerging. So, while you should concentrate your efforts on stores specializing in crafts, you should also be on the lookout for other possible sites where you might sell your work.

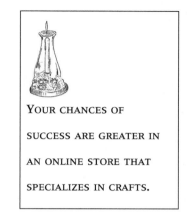

YOUR CHANCES OF SUCCESS ARE GREATER IN AN ONLINE STORE THAT SPECIALIZES IN CRAFTS.

Some online craft stores offer a basic, catalog-type display of products with photographs and accompanying descriptions; a prospective customer must contact the vendor by mail, phone, fax, or e-mail to place an order. Other stores accept orders, which they forward to the craftsperson. Still others offer fully interactive sites where the customer places the order online, makes payment by credit card over a secure server, and the craftsperson is sent a check (usually once a month) by the store.

Finding the best online store for your product is similar in some ways to finding the best brick-and-mortar shop, but there are some different things to look for in the online world. The following is a list of 12 questions you should ask of any online store, whether or not it specializes in crafts. How you rank these 12 questions in order of importance will depend partly on the kind of product you make and partly on the amount of online business you want to generate. If, for example, you make one-of-a-kind pieces, you may want to put questions 5 and 6 at the top of your list. If you want to conduct a lot of your business online, then questions 8 and 9 may rank closer to the top of your list. But whatever ranking you assign to these questions, all 12 of them need to be answered before you can find the best online store for your work.

1. What does the store offer?

Does the store provide only exposure for your products, or does it have an ordering system with transactions through a secure server? How many products can you put into the store? How easy is it for you to add products or make changes? If the store makes sales, how are orders filled? Does the store have a facility for holding an inventory of goods or (as is more usual with online stores) do you ship directly to the customer? How are sales reported to you and how are you paid?

2. How much does it cost?

Cost varies widely, depending on what is being offered. Some sites charge a monthly fee based on the number of pages taken up by your products. This can be as little as $4.95 per page (with usually five photographs per page), but you can expect to pay considerably more if the site offers features such as secure online transactions. Other sites operate on the basis of commissions (typically 20 percent) on sales. In some cases there is a set-up fee as well.

3. How easy is it to find?

Try finding the site on the most popular search engines — AltaVista, Excite, Hotbot, Infoseek, Lycos, Magellan, MSN, Yahoo, and Webcrawler. Does it appear among the first ten or fifteen sites in the list? If not, then it will not be found by most users doing a general Web search and would probably not be a good place to sell your work.

4. Does the site download quickly and easily?

If a visitor has to wait too long for a site to download, he or she is likely to go somewhere else. How long is too long? There is no hard and fast rule since download speeds vary widely, depending on how a user is connected. But Internet users in general have a bias towards speed. One study showed that the amount of time between clicks for the average Web surfer was seven seconds!

5. How are products presented?

There are a number of things to look for, including the following:

- photographs should be high quality
- design work should be clean and crisp, so that everything is clear at a glance
- site should be easy to navigate
- crafts should be accessible within one or two mouse clicks
- ordering methods should be clear and easy
- refund policy should be clearly stated

6. What kinds of products are offered for sale?

You should look for vendors who offer products that are compatible with yours. If you are looking for craft stores, you should be aware that some sites promote themselves as craft sites but sell many different kinds of merchandise, including mass-market goods, craft supplies and kits, and cheap souvenir items. If you make custom furniture, for example, you would not want to have your products in a store that offers mainly low-priced souvenirs. Some online craft sites sell only genuinely handcrafted items and have very specific standards. Some sites will sell virtually anything to make a buck. Some online stores have written policies on standards and the quality of work they will accept. If you are concerned about quality, look not just at their policies but at the actual products they are selling on their site.

7. How many vendors are represented on the site?

Generally, the more the better. In an online craft store, you should look for balance in the kinds of crafts being offered; too many in one particular medium may limit the appeal of the site for potential buyers.

8. How much traffic is there?

In the real world a store's location is extremely important. Everyone has heard the old cliché: the three most important things in retailing are location, location, and location. Location is so important because it is the key to traffic. It is the same on the Web, except that it is not physical location that is important but the amount of traffic that finds its way to the site.

Many online vendors will tell you how much traffic there is in their stores in terms of how many hits there are on their sites. Some sites have counters on the home pages that show visitors the number of hits. Be aware, though, of what these numbers really mean. The hits represent the number of times the server on which the Web site is located sends information to a visitor. Sometimes these numbers sound very impressive. But the figures can be misleading because each component of a page — text, pictures, or any other file — is counted as a hit. If, for example, a person looks at a Web page with five pictures on it, the number of hits would be counted as six (five images plus the text of the page itself).

There are other rates of measurement for Web traffic. Web servers also record page views, where each page is counted as a separate entity, so that when someone looks at a page it counts only once instead of once for each component file that the page contains. Inaccuracies can arise here, too, because some Web browsers store the entire contents of a page for a limited amount of time. If a visitor to a site requests a page and then later returns to the same page, the browser may not request the page from the Web server, but may retrieve it from memory instead.

A Web server can also store information about a visitor to a site on the visitor's hard drive in what is known as a cookie file. Both the

Netscape and Internet Explorer browsers have files for the storage of cookies. The Web server has the ability to look inside a computer's cookie file and read the stored information. Cookies can store all kinds of information, including unique numbers for each visitor, which allows online merchants to determine (among other things) the total number of visitors to their site. But this method of counting has its drawbacks too, because users can turn off the cookie function in their browsers so that their computers will not accept cookies from the Web server.

All measurements of a site's traffic have limitations. Still, it is better to have a rough guide rather than none at all. Your best bet is to look for a traffic counter on the main page, and take this number with a grain of salt. If there is no traffic counter, this may indicate that the company does not want the number of visitors known.

Traffic on the Web does not necessarily translate into sales. To be successful, a store has to generate not just traffic, but sales. Visitors have to be turned into customers, then into repeat customers. There is no infallible way of knowing beforehand whether an online store can do this for your product. Contacting other craftspeople who sell through the store might provide a good indication.

9. How is the store promoted?

Does the site have an advertising budget? If so, the owners will sometimes tell you how much they spend on advertising. How and where do they place their ads? Do they rely on Internet-based advertising, such as links with other sites and banner ads (for a discussion of these techniques, see the section "Promoting Your Web Site" below), or do they advertise in other media?

10. How long has the store been in business?

Many on-line stores have only been in operation for a year or two; some have been around longer. Being new is not necessarily a bad thing. If there is no track record by which the store might be judged, you can ask the owner about his or her objectives and goals for the site.

11. Who owns and administers the store?

Some online stores are run by people with retail experience in the real world. The owners of online craft stores may have sold crafts in actual craft fairs. Other sites may be run by people with experience in

Web development or design. Generally, extensive retail experience is a good sign that the sites' owners know a thing or two about marketing. Sometimes the owner will describe his or her background on the Web site; if not, you can always ask before you make any decision.

12. Does the store inspire trust?

Trust is, of course, very difficult to measure, but it is extremely important that potential online shoppers trust the Web site. Shopping online is still a relatively new phenomenon, and many people are cautious, especially when it comes to giving out their addresses or credit card information. Don't be afraid to ask the site owners for references. Check with other craftspeople who have used the site.

(A list of online craft stores and Internet malls appears in Appendix 3.)

d. Should You Have Your Own Online Store?

There are a variety of reasons why you might prefer to have your own online store. Even if you are selling your products on someone else's Web site, you might wish to have your own distinctive presence on the Web. Perhaps you want to be more in control of how your work is sold. Or you may want to shift a substantial part of your marketing from more traditional craft outlets and make a major commitment to online sales and customer relations.

It is not difficult to set up a Web site of your own, but it takes more time and effort, and it costs substantially more than selling in someone else's online store. If you decide to have your own online store, there are three basic options:

(i) You can use a ready-to-go online storefront.

(ii) You can build your own online store.

(iii) You can hire a professional Web developer to build an online store for you.

The choice here depends essentially on the following two areas of consideration:

(i) How much time and money you do you wish to spend and what is your level of design and computer skill? There is inexpensive software available which allows virtually anyone to build a site and post it to the Web. But it still takes a substantial commitment of time and effort to achieve a satisfactory result.

(ii) What kind of site do you want? Do you want merely to put your products in an online brochure? Much like a conventional paper brochure, this gives you the opportunity to advertise your work and tell people how to get in touch with you. It puts your company's message on the Internet 24 hours a day, 7 days a week. With a bit of effort, everyone is capable of creating an online brochure. Or do you wish to have a full-blown e-commerce site, at which customers can input their requirements for customized work and make direct purchases using credit cards or account numbers? Aside from design skills, such a site requires database and Web-page generation software, in addition to credit card authentication and authorization software for the secure transmission of sensitive information. Unless you have design and programming skills, you are probably better off hiring someone to do the job for you. You can use one of the many full-service electronic storefronts or Internet malls, or you can hire the services of a professional to build your own site.

e. Online Stores and Internet Malls

There are many companies offering full-service electronic storefronts, including Web-site design, online shopping carts, full ordering capability, Web-site hosting, domain registration, and Web-site promotion. Many of these companies offer everything you need for a full-fledged, online commerce operation under one roof.

Yahoo! Store is one of the best known. For $150 per month, you can have an online store with up to 50 items and a full array of e-commerce features, including Web-site generation, product search, online shopping cart, and site promotion. This is about as easy as e-commerce gets. There are many other quality storefront generators on the Web. Many — though not all — offer a full range of e-commerce features. Costs vary widely; some do not charge fees but rely instead on a commission on the products sold by their clients.

Internet malls offer many of the same services as the electronic storefronts. You could think of an Internet mall as somewhat analogous to a real mall, where you rent or lease a separate store (Web site)

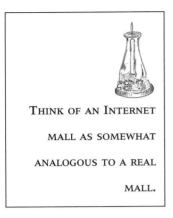

in a building containing other stores (linked Web sites). Online craft malls generally provide you with your own out-of-the-box Web site with a variety of e-commerce options, including shopping cart, secure ordering, hosting, and domain registration. Prices start as low as $49 for basic packages.

Usually your mall site is registered under the Internet address of the mall (e.g., <www.onebigmall.com/yourname>), but some on-line malls allow you to register your own Internet address (e.g., <www.yourname.com>). Some will even take care of the registration for you. Having your own Internet address costs a bit more but it may be worth it in the long run if you are serious about selling on the Net. Recent surveys of online shopping show that customers almost invariably trust a site more when it has its own domain name (often referred to as a URL or Uniform Resource Locator). Also, some search engines may not find you if you do not have your own Internet address.

Next to selling your crafts in someone else's online store, this is the fastest and easiest way to get your work on the Internet. But is it the best way? This depends on your objectives. If you want your own online store, but you have limited computer skills and a very limited amount of time to commit to the project, this might be your best choice.

f. Your Own Web Site

If you decide to build your own Web site or hire someone to build it for you, it is imperative that you begin with a clear plan as to what you expect the site to do for your business. You should be able to answer the following questions before you begin:

- How do you do business now and how do you plan to do business in the future?
- Do you rely on crafts shows, wholesaling your work to shops, mail order, or a combination of these?
- Do you want to increase business with your existing clientele or to reach new customers?
- Are you aiming your online marketing efforts at wholesale or retail clients, or both? What stage are you at in your current craft business?
- Are you planning to start up a new craft business on the Web?

How much time and money are you prepared to spend?

How are you going to maintain your site?

Once your site is up and running, it will require updating and maintenance on a regular basis. This takes time. If you want people to return to your site, you have to keep it fresh and interesting, free of technical glitches, and up-to-date. Few people will want to revisit a site that looks the same all the time.

A plan for going online does not need to be a formal printed document in a hard-cover binder. It can be as simple as a list of steps to be taken, handwritten on a piece of plain paper. (It does help to put it down in writing, no matter how short.) A well-conceived plan will involve defining your goals and objectives, deciding the kind of online presence you want, and determining how best to achieve it. It should also include a marketing plan, outlining how you will promote your site once it is up and running.

A detailed plan does not mean that your online enterprise is guaranteed to succeed, but you can be certain that without a plan you will run a high risk of failure. There are many spectacular success stories of businesses, large and small, that have gone online; there are also stories of companies of all sizes that have invested heavily in the Net with little to show for it.

Once you have a plan, you will be in a position to draw up a set of objectives to define exactly what your Web site will do. Suppose, for example, you want to increase sales by 20 percent to 25 percent by finding new customers outside your conventional marketing outlets (craft shows and shops). You want customers to be able to order products directly from your site and you want to increase sales from your existing customers by getting them to visit your site.

These objectives define the features your site should have. There are a number of factors to consider when clarifying the objectives of your Web site. Some of the most important ones are discussed below.

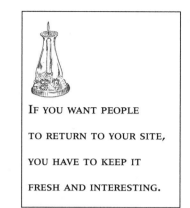

IF YOU WANT PEOPLE TO RETURN TO YOUR SITE, YOU HAVE TO KEEP IT FRESH AND INTERESTING.

(a) Photographs of your products

Do you also want to include other photographs, such as pictures of yourself or the area where you work? Remember, you should aim to make your site as interesting as possible.

(b) Product information

How do you deliver information on prices, product specs, and ordering to your customers? Will a catalog-type listing suffice, or do you want a search capability?

(c) Customer information

How much information do you want to collect from your customers beyond name, address, and shipping information? Do you want to be able to build a database of customer preferences for specific products?

(d) Contact information

Do you want an online form that customers can fill out? Do you want them to e-mail you? Or do you want to use a fax or a 1-800 number instead?

(e) Purchasing

Do you want customers to be able to make purchases on the site? If so, you will need a shopping cart. This is a piece of software that works much the way it sounds; it allows customers to pick out items from your site and keep track of what they have selected by putting them into a virtual shopping cart. When they are ready to purchase, they then fill out the order form with their address and credit card information. (Without a shopping cart, this information would have to be entered for each and every selection.)

(f) Transactions

If you want customers to make financial transactions on the site, you will need credit card authorization and authentication software. To accept credit cards for online sales, you will need to have a special form of merchant account, called a card not present (CNP) account. If you already have a merchant account with your bank, you should ask them about getting a CNP account. If you do not have a merchant credit card account, it is best to approach your own bank first and ask if they offer CNP accounts.

(g) Security

What kind of security features will you need? If you are accepting credit cards online, you will need to have your site hosted on a secure server. The most commonly used security system at present (SSL) relies on the encryption of information that flows between a browser and a Web site. You do not need to know anything about the inner workings of this technology (which is built into most Web browsers) in order to use it.

g. Building Your Web Site

Many software packages are available for building your own Web site. These programs are usually referred to as Web page generators or HTML editors because they generate the HTML (short for Hyper-Text Markup Language) code that is used to build Web pages. There are dozens of excellent HTML editors available — some are even free, and can be downloaded at <www.tucows.com>, a site that also provides Web design tutorials. Some well-known site building programs include the following:

MANY SOFTWARE PACKAGES ARE AVAILABLE FOR BUILDING YOUR OWN WEB SITE.

- Adobe GoLive (www.adobe.com)
- FileMaker Home Page (www.filemakerpro.com)
- Macromedia Dreamweaver (www.macromedia.com)
- Microsoft FrontPage (www.microsoft.com)

Most of these programs work on the what-you-see-is-what-you-get principle, known as WYSIWYG. (Computer types dearly love acronyms, even ones you can't pronounce!) What this really means is that you don't have to understand computer code to know where things will end up on the page, and you can see the final version take shape on your screen as you go along.

No matter which software you use, the Web-building process should proceed through the following three stages:

1. Design

Starting with the objectives you derived from your business plan, you design the layout and navigation of your site. It often helps to look at other sites on the Web for ideas; look for sites that are easy to navigate and have attractive and pleasing designs. Lay your site out on paper (yes, plain old-fashioned paper!); first a page layout, then a flowchart or diagram of the various pages and how they will be linked together.

Think of the flowchart as the blueprint for your site. Mark the areas where you intend to put your photographs and graphics. Put in every bit of content, every navigation bar and interactive component, and remember that everything on your site must work well together. Try to put yourself in the place of a prospective customer or visitor to your site as you go over the main elements of site design.

Pay particular attention to navigation and content organization. The typical method of navigating around a site is by means of a navigation bar with graphic icons or boxes that hyper-link to different content sections of the Web. Make certain that visitors can easily get back to your home page no matter where they are on your site. Group content into distinct areas and arrange these areas logically, checking to see that each link connects to the appropriate page. You should construct an organizational chart showing all the content for the Web site on a single sheet of paper.

With such highly visual products as crafts, you should strive for a clear focus on the products themselves. You want a clean, uncluttered layout, without distracting elements that divide the focus of the eye. You want to make it as easy as possible for a visitor to get to the actual products; they should be no more than one or two mouse clicks away from your home page.

Color and typography are also important to your site. Don't use colors or patterns that distract the eye's focus. For many handcrafted items, the best background is one that is close to the color of the page itself so that the object appears to be standing right on the page. There are thousands of different fonts available. For best effects use just one or two primary fonts which you can vary by size, color, or by bolding or italicizing some words.

2. Graphics

You can use a scanner to convert conventional photographs to digital images that can be put on your computer. Or, if you are using a digital camera, you can simply transfer the images to your computer using the software that comes with your camera. If you are scanning pictures, use only originals of the highest quality; a scan will not correct any deficiencies in a picture. Because of the importance of visual imagery in presenting crafts, you may want to consider having your photographs taken by a professional.

There are a number of possible image formats for the Web, but the JPEG format (short for Joint Photographic Experts Group) is best for high-resolution photographs in which gradations of color are important. Images can be stored in a variety of resolutions; the one you use will involve a trade-off between quality and file size. Too large a file size will mean too long a download time — something you want to avoid. It is also important not to present full-size images of your products until your visitors request them. Use smaller, thumbnail images that visitors can click on if they want to see more.

3. Moving your site to the Web

In many cases it is possible to have your site hosted by your Internet Service Provider (ISP), and it is worth checking into this possibility before you look elsewhere. Some ISPs even provide a limited amount of free Web space to their subscribers. This free space, which is often used for small personal sites (between 5 and 10 megabytes), may be a good place to accommodate an online brochure. Even if you plan a larger, more sophisticated, commercial site, you might want to try out one of these free sites in order to get a feel for the site-building process before you buy more Web space.

THERE ARE THOUSANDS OF COMPANIES THAT WILL HOST YOUR WEB SITE; PRICES AND SERVICE LEVELS VARY WIDELY

There are thousands of companies that will host your Web site; prices and service levels vary widely. You can pay as little as $20 per month for basic hosting. If you need database or interactive applications, expect to pay considerably more. To find a suitable company, you might begin with these resources:

- the *Yellow Pages*
- Web directories
- chamber of commerce listings
- www.findwebspace.com

Before you sign up, ask the hosting company about the availability of server log analysis software. These programs allow you to generate all kinds of useful statistics about your site, including the following:

- the average time visitors spend on your site
- the sites from which visitors reached your site
- the keywords that were used to find your site on a search engine

Such information is invaluable in Web marketing, and if you plan to do your own online promotion, you should use a hosting service that will provide this kind of data.

Some hosting companies will also look after the registration of your domain name. The Domain Name System (DNS) is what allows users to find their way around the Internet. Every computer has a unique number, known as its IP (Internet Protocol) address, a long string of numbers separated by dots. The DNS allows an easily recognizable string of letters, called the domain name, to be used instead of the number string.

Registering a domain name (or URL) gives you an entry in a directory of all the domain names and their corresponding computers on the Internet. You can pick almost any name you like, provided that it is not already taken. If at all possible, choose a name that is descriptive of your business. For detailed information on the process of registering your domain name, and the meaning of the various types of addresses (such as .com, .org, .biz and so on) visit InterNIC (the Internet Network Information Centre) at <www.internic.net/faqs>.

It is not difficult to move your new Web site to the host server. Many Web-page generation packages have a built-in component (called an FTP or file transfer protocol client) that allows you to upload or publish your site to the server. If your software doesn't have an FTP client, you can download one free from the Internet. (See <www.tucows.com>.)

Once your site is up and running, you will want to test it to make certain that everything works as planned before you launch into the next stage: promotion. Remember, building your site is only half the job; the other half is building traffic and sales.

h. Hiring a Web Developer to Build Your Site

Hiring a professional to build your site does not mean that you hand over the job over to someone else and then sit back and wait for the results. A good Web-site developer knows how to build an online store, and a professional marketer can show you ways to get people to visit your store once you get it on the Web. But nobody knows your business as well as you do; nobody can build a good site for you unless your input is an integral part of the process.

How much does it cost to have a professional build and maintain your site? This is a question that is impossible to answer in the abstract. Obviously, a Web developer offering his or her services for a $99 dollar set-up fee and $19.95 per month is providing something different from someone who quotes you $3,500 for set-up, plus monthly fees of $150. The lower fee might get you a bare bones site with pictures of your products, plus descriptions. For the higher quote you would expect more, perhaps a search and database capability, eye-catching graphics, and/or secure transaction features. It all depends on what you want. This is why it is so important to plan your site before you hire a developer.

With your site plan in hand, you will be able to put together a request for a proposal (RFP). You should always get at least three quotes from different Web developers before you make a final decision as to who will build your site. Unless you draw up a clear RFP, it will be difficult to compare different proposals. One company may be proposing an online catalog; another may be quoting on an e-commerce site with secure transaction features.

Look for a developer in your own area. You don't want to pay the travel expenses for someone from another town or city and you will need to work closely with the person you hire to build your site. Ask for references and take the time to check them out, as well as to look at sites the developer has recently completed.

Draw up a written contract that spells out exactly what you want in your site. Don't think that this is too much trouble; instead, think of it as a way of avoiding possible trouble. If you were hiring a contractor to rewire your home or to install a new heating system, you would want a written agreement. Putting together a custom-built Web site is a complex process. It makes good business sense to make certain that everyone knows exactly what is expected.

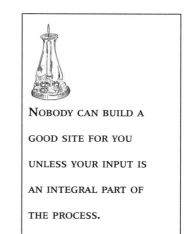

NOBODY CAN BUILD A GOOD SITE FOR YOU UNLESS YOUR INPUT IS AN INTEGRAL PART OF THE PROCESS.

i. Promoting Your Site

The Web is a highly interactive medium. This is a fact that cannot be stressed often enough if you are considering building and maintaining your own Web site. A site needs regular maintenance. This means keeping the site up and running, monitoring it regularly, and solving any technical problems or glitches no matter what time of the day or night they occur. It also means keeping your site interesting. This takes time, effort, and some skill if you plan on doing the work yourself.

Remember what we said about repeat business in the earlier chapters on traditional craft marketing channels. Your goal is not just to get a customer to visit your booth or the shop selling your products; you want customers to buy and you want them to come back again. Similarly, if you want first-time visitors to your Web site to return, you have to give them a reason to do so. If the information on your Web site never seems to change, there is little reason for a customer to visit it again. As often as possible, announce new products, provide information on upcoming craft shows, and use your imagination to think of other ways to encourage customers to return to your site.

There are a number of tried and proven methods of building traffic to your site:

1. Use your domain name as much as possible

One of the best ways of advertising your site is to include your domain name (i.e., <www.myowncraftshop.com>) on all your business cards, letterhead, brochures, craft show listings — indeed, anywhere you can. Include it in all your correspondence and in any kind of advertising you do in whatever medium (newspaper, magazine, radio, etc.) you use.

2. Submit your site to search engines

One of the biggest sources of traffic is Web searches, but this does not mean that you need to submit your site to hundreds of search engines. It is sufficient to submit to the major eight: AltaVista, Excite, Hotbot, Infoseek, Lycos, MSN, WebCrawler, and Yahoo. Use the information found on their pages to make certain your registration is accurate and complete. If you wish to register your site with some of the many smaller search engines, you can save a lot of time by using an online registration service that will make multiple submissions in your name. For more information on search engines, go to <www.searchenginewatch.com>.

3. Optimize the position of your site

If a site does not appear among the top ten or fifteen listings returned by a search engine, it is not likely to be found by many users. For this reason, Web developers spend a lot of time finding ways to optimize the position of their sites in searches. You can find an enormous amount of information on this subject on the Web itself — far more than can be briefly summarized here. There is no single method of ensuring that your site will rank in the top ten or fifteen sites listed because all search engines are different and search methodologies change from time to time. But if you are serious about promoting your site, it is worth your while to spend some time exploring this subject. Again, a good place to start is <www.searchenginewatch.com>.

4. Get links from related sites

Having links to your site from related sites can have a significant impact on the amount of traffic you receive. To get a link from a related site, ask the site administrator or Webmaster. Briefly describe your site and explain why you think the link would be advantageous. (You will usually find the e-mail address of the site administrator or Webmaster near the bottom of a site's home page.) Often, you will be asked for a link in return. Choose your links carefully; a link can siphon off traffic as well as bring in traffic. Check to make certain that the site to which you will link has standards compatible with your own.

There are Web sites that specialize in establishing links for artists and craftspeople. Begin with the following:

- Artseek Internet Art Resource Directory at <www.artseek.com>
- Electronic Cottage Gallery at <www.electroniccottage.com>
- CraftWEB Project at <www.craftweb.com>

5. Advertise on the Net

Another way to promote your site is to buy banner ads on the Internet. These have the advantage of making it very easy for a customer to get to your site. They are also easy to create, using online tools that allow you to design your own ad. The drawbacks are that they are expensive and, even if they bring lots of visitors to your site, there is nothing to guarantee that these visitors will place orders. As with traditional advertising, you pay each time your ad is shown. Each appearance of your ad is called an impression, and companies often quote prices per thousand impressions. The more popular the site, the higher the price a company can charge for banner advertising.

The effectiveness of banner advertising is the subject of some debate in Web marketing circles. One study suggests that a banner ad will be clicked only once in 22 appearances. Most craftspeople would be well advised to wait until they have a feel for the numbers of buyers they are actually getting from visitors to their site before they spend money on banner ads.

6. Make your site sticky

What is it that makes a Web site able to attract and hold visitors, and makes them want to return to the site? Web marketers refer to this quality as stickiness. The stickiness of a site comes from the interaction of three elements:

(1) content: what is on the site and how it is presented

(2) interface: how quickly and easily the site downloads and how easy it is to use and navigate

(3) add-ons: complimentary services that visitors to a site find useful and interesting (i.e., a calendar of upcoming craft shows or arts events)

Carefully consider these three elements and determine how you can improve them in your own site.

j. Making Your Work Easy to Buy

There are a number of things you can do to make your work sell, in addition to designing and building an attractive Web site, building traffic, and having good products and prices. The following three strategies will improve the ease with which customers may buy your products.

1. Offer choices

The Internet is all about choice. Offer a selection of your products in various sizes, styles, and prices, but don't offer such a wide range that it becomes confusing. Offer prospective customers as many ordering options as possible: mail, phone, fax, e-mail, and online order form. Offer more than one payment option: credit card, check in advance, even C.O.D. if you are just starting out. (Think carefully about C.O.D., however, because there can be drawbacks to it. For example, if shipments are refused by an addressee, you could be stuck with freight charges and extra paperwork.)

2. Make everything crystal clear

Your Web site should allow no room for confusion. Ensure that the following is clearly stated:

- how a prospective customer can contact you

- when the product will be shipped

- by what method the product will be shipped

Be certain to make this information easy to find on your site.

3. Make yourself real

This is one of the most important components of all. You want prospective customers to be comfortable shopping in your online store; you want them to feel that your company is solid, reliable, and trustworthy. (Even ING Direct, the global financial conglomerate, reminds prospective online clients that there is a real bank behind the virtual one.) Make your company real by giving a real civic address and by showing a picture of yourself, your workshop, or your retail outlet — whichever is most photogenic — on your Web site.

YOUR WEB SITE SHOULD ALLOW NO ROOM FOR CONFUSION.

k. The Future of Online Shopping for Crafts

Several of the major search engines, including MSN and Yahoo, have set up specific areas of the Internet just for shopping. Some Web consultants predict that in the long run, these huge Internet hubs, offering one-stop shopping in dozens of categories, are the places where shoppers will go to look for products online. But the Internet is evolving very rapidly and no one can say for certain that this will be the case.

For most artists and craftspeople, the results from big online shopping hubs have been disappointing. There is, moreover, something of a catch-22 situation here for most craftspeople. If sales from one of these malls really took off, they would be incapable of producing the quantities of goods required. At this point in the evolution of the Net, most artists and craftspeople have had the best results from online craft stores or their own Web sites.

l. Wholesaling Your Work Online

If you sell your work online, either on your own Web site or through an online store or mall, it is possible that owners of stores and galleries may come across your products and get in touch with you. It is not that much different from craft shows; craftspeople are often approached at shows by store owners looking for new and interesting products to sell in their stores. But most craftspeople who are serious about wholesaling don't restrict their wholesale marketing efforts to chance meetings with store owners at craft shows. They will almost certainly pursue one or more of the strategies discussed in Chapter 6 for getting their work into shops.

It is the same on the Net. If you want to use your Web site as a \wholesale marketing tool, you have to develop a strategy. One

obvious way is to have a link on your Web site that will take wholesale customers to a separate page or part of the site dealing with wholesale. There are, however, drawbacks to this. If you have detailed wholesale information, including wholesale prices, available on your site, you won't likely want retail customers going to that part of your site — and you can be almost certain that your wholesale customers won't want it either. You wouldn't leave your wholesale price list lying on display at a craft show!

One way of tackling this is to have different products in the wholesale section of your Web site, things that you don't offer at retail prices. Another option is to have a password to your wholesale Web pages; you would only give out this password to your wholesale customers. Large manufacturing companies sometimes provide a link to a separate section of their Web site with access by password for bona fide resellers. If you require a password for the wholesale part of your site, you will need some way of luring prospective wholesale customers (shops, galleries, etc.) to your site and getting them to fill out an online application form. All this can become quite complicated for a small craft business.

A simpler solution is to use the services of an online crafts wholesaler. (See Appendix 3.) You can put pictures of your products on display, along with descriptive text, much like an online retail store. The owners of the wholesale store would promote the site to retailers who could visit and place orders. How well this would work for you would depend on a number of things, including the amount of promotion done by the wholesale site and the kind of product you are selling.

There are not very many online craft wholesalers at present; to find a good one you would want to ask the same twelve questions discussed in section "c" of this chapter.

m. How Craft Businesses Have Fared on the Web

A few craftspeople went online early, starting in the mid-1990s when the Internet began to gain in popularity. But most craftspeople currently online have had an online presence for less than two years. For this reason, hard statistics of online craft sales have to be treated with some caution. Still, certain conclusions can be drawn. According to a recent survey by the magazine *Crafts Report*, some craftspeople are indeed making money on the Internet, but not all. The *Crafts Report* study was unable to say definitively why some craftspeople succeeded online where others failed, though it suggested that staying power (the longer one is online, the better one's chances) and promotion are important factors. Obviously, the quality and appeal of the product are major considerations as well.

n. Three Keys to Online Success

There is no single, overriding factor that determines whether your Web-based venture will make money. But mounting evidence from recent research into online merchandising suggests there are three keys to success:

(i) A good business plan

Launching a Web site without a good business plan just might bring in some money. But the odds are against it; it will more likely only cost you time and money.

(ii) A top-quality presentation

If you are selling a quality product, you have to display it on a top-quality Web site, whether your own site or someone else's.

(iii) Continuous promotion

Having a good business plan and a top-quality presentation on a first-rate Web site does not mean you can sit back and expect the money to come pouring in. The Web site — your own or the one carrying your products — needs to be actively and continuously promoted. In a nutshell, this means work and someone has to do it — you, your employee, or the person responsible for running the online store.

Chapter 8

MARKETING TIPS

a. Start Out Close to Home

Tackle the easiest market first. Bear in mind at all times the cost of shipping your goods to market, getting sales, and maintaining contact with your customers. Generally, you will start out in your own town or city and gradually expand sales to other parts of your state or province. There may be a booming market for hand-dipped candles on the east coast, but if you are a candlemaker on the west coast, it's better to establish yourself at home first before you try shipping your work across the continent.

This doesn't mean that you should turn down an opportunity to sell your work just because the customer is in a distant part of the country. A friend of mine making handmade clothing in New England got her first big wholesale order from a shop in Alaska.

The Internet is changing the way many goods and services are sold. For some products (e.g., computer software and music) these changes are dramatic, for others less so. For still others, the impact of the Net remains to be seen. But it does offer small businesses a direct channel to customers anywhere in the world, and if you can take advantage of it to sell your work, you should do so. There is no inherent reason why you could not make your first marketing efforts on the

Net, though the experience of most craft businesses to date suggests that this is not the easiest place to start.

b. Find Your Own Niche in the Market

Try to find a niche of your own in the marketplace. The possibilities in the craft world are so diverse that it is possible to develop your own particular products. If you are a potter, you may become known for a certain kind of miniature; if you work in leather, you may specialize in painting on your work; if you make sweaters, you may use unique designs.

With experience, you will learn just how long you can keep a good-selling item on the market. You shouldn't take a good seller out of production just because it has been around for a while, but, on the other hand, don't get into a rut and flog a product in the market after it has passed its peak. Keep your line fresh by introducing new products regularly. Be prepared to follow shifts in consumer tastes and demands.

c. Aim for the Highest Quality

Exhibit and offer for sale only your best work. Don't try to sell any of your seconds, (i.e., work that is flawed in any way), until you have an established reputation for quality work. One of the privileges of being established is that your seconds will find a market. But sell them only as seconds, at a reduced price, and in an appropriate marketplace. If you are selling at a craft market, check with the organizers to see if they have any objections to the sale of seconds.

d. Avoid Saturating a Particular Market

Most craft products sell best in a given market area when the quantities available in that market are below the saturation point. The saturation point is the point at which the product begins to lose its appeal because there is, or appears to be, too much of it on the market. Many handcrafted products are vulnerable to market saturation. They are different from other commodities because of their aesthetic appeal and because the consumer places a special value on handmade, unique goods. Some people may be "turned off" a product if it seems that "everyone has it."

In most cases, the saturation point is well beyond the production limits of the individual craftworker, so it is not really a constraint on

BE PREPARED TO FOLLOW

SHIFTS IN CONSUMER

TASTES AND DEMANDS.

sales. In other words, unless a market area is very small or very thinly populated or there are many competitors producing the same product, most craftworkers can sell virtually all they are capable of producing. If there is any danger of market saturation in your home town, you can expand sales by attending out-of-town craft shows, by selling to shops in other areas, going to trade shows, or selling your work on the Internet. If you have a really hot product with a high saturation point, you may want to expand your business by hiring people to work for you. If you are capable of producing a large quantity of product, avoid overselling it in any given market area.

For instance, George and Susan had a successful stained glass business, selling their work to a variety of quality craft and gift shops in the New England area. In just a few years, they had built up their business to the point where they employed half a dozen full-time workers and a number of part-time ones. Although they made a variety of different stained glass products, their lamp shades were the most popular and accounted for a large part of their business.

George, who was very ambitious, wanted to expand into some of the major gift and department stores. He hired several additional workers and went after some large accounts. He was successful in getting initial orders for lamp shades from a number of department stores, including one with a mail-order catalog operation.

At first George and Susan were elated. Then something happened that neither had foreseen. Some of their smaller accounts stopped ordering because they didn't want to handle products that were being sold by big department stores in their neighborhood. Soon, other stores dropped away too. Some were leery of selling products that were available from a major mail-order company, and others claimed that demand for the lamp shades had fallen off. George and Susan became increasingly dependent on a few large customers. Within two years, they were forced to cut back drastically and to lay off most of their workers when several of their biggest customers failed to repeat their orders.

George and Susan had oversold their work. Their lamp shades were original and appealing, but the appeal was to the kind of customer who wanted something different, the discriminating buyer who sought a product that was not available everywhere. Once the product even appeared to be everywhere, it lost much of its appeal.

There are a number of ways in which George and Susan could have overcome their problems. If they had diversified and sold a different kind of lamp shade to the big stores, they may have been able to keep their small customers as well. Or they could have introduced new items into the bigger stores under a different name and kept their regular line moving in the smaller gift and craft shops. Another option would have been to promote their existing products outside the New England area by engaging sales representatives or by attending trade shows in other parts of the country.

e. Build Customer Loyalty

Be loyal to your existing customers. You appreciate their loyalty to you, so remember to return their trust. If you have a good account in a particular area, don't open another that is in direct competition with the first. Say you are selling $2,000 worth of products every summer to the ABC Store in the resort town of Bubbling Brook. If you open up another account in the town, you may find that you still have just $2,000 worth of business in Bubbling Brook, but now it is divided between the ABC Store and your new account.

ALWAYS ASK YOUR CUSTOMERS BEFOREHAND WHETHER OR NOT THEY WANT TO RECEIVE INFORMATION FROM YOU.

Service your accounts well. Even if you have a sales representative who makes regular calls, it is a good idea to keep your customers posted about developments in your business. When you introduce new products, send out a photograph or brochure. If you have to increase your prices, give your customers plenty of advance notice and explain why the increase is necessary. Be prompt to replace any items short-shipped or defective.

If you have your own Web site, be certain to keep it up to date. Even if you do not sell your work online, you can still use the Internet to keep in touch with your customers by sending them e-mails to announce new products or upcoming craft shows. But be careful how you do this. No-one likes to have their mailbox filled with junk mail, and many people define junk mail as anything they didn't ask for. Always ask your customers beforehand whether or not they want to receive information from you, and always give them a way of telling you to stop sending it.

Filling the initial order with a shop or gallery is just the beginning; repeat orders are the best measure of your success in the marketplace. What you want is an active repeat business. Once you are established in the market, a large part of your business will be repeats.

If a shop or gallery is a good account, stick with it. Try to increase your sales in a particular area by increasing your sales to an existing account before you consider opening another account. Of course, this is not always possible. There may be accounts that will buy a certain amount of your work and no more. These stores may feature other kinds of work and they may not want to shift their focus too much towards any particular craft.

When you sell to craft shops and galleries, try to get your work featured if possible. Many retailers have a relatively small number of items that account for a sizable proportion of their sales. These are the items that are displayed in their front windows and in the most prominent places inside the shop and are featured in their advertisements. Sales of your work in a particular shop can depend on how your products are displayed and promoted by the shop. Once your products are seen to be good sellers, store owners will naturally give them increased prominence. In the beginning, you have to rely on the appeal of your products to the store owner and your own persuasiveness to get your work prominently displayed.

If a shop is obliged to order a certain minimum quantity of your products each time, this helps ensure that more of your work is displayed. A minimum order policy is also helpful in keeping your paperwork costs down. It may not be possible or wise to require a minimum order when you are starting out. Store owners who are not familiar with your work may be unwilling to buy any more than one or two pieces to test the market. However, as soon as you find that your work is selling, you should insist on a minimum order.

It's not uncommon for a shop to want to be the exclusive outlet for your product in a given area. There is nothing inherently wrong with an exclusive arrangement, provided that the shop is able to realize the potential for sales of your products in that area. When you are starting out, it is difficult to know potential sales, so be careful with any exclusive arrangement and keep it initially to a relatively short period of time.

f.   Set Realistic Marketing Goals

Be patient. Rome wasn't built in a day. You have to work hard to build up a clientele. Set realistic marketing goals. Remember, it took time to perfect your production techniques and it will take time to work out a successful marketing system. The thing to be concerned about at any given point in the development of your business is not so much the actual volume of your sales but the trend of sales and whether or not it is steadily increasing.

If you decide to launch a new marketing initiative (i.e., to show your work at a trade show in another city or to put your work on the Internet) you should allow sufficient time for your efforts to bear fruit. Don't pull out of a prospective market just because first-time sales at a new show were less than you expected. It could be that you were in the wrong show for your type of product, or the new market takes time to develop.

PUBLICITY IS, IN ESSENCE, FREE ADVERTISING.

An example can be made of a fellow craftsperson, a producer of hand-made children's clothing who is successful at craft shows in a number of different cities. A few years ago, she tried selling her work in another major city and she barely managed to cover her expenses. She would have abandoned her plans for the new market altogether had a friend not suggested she try selling some of her more expensive items at a smaller, juried show just before Christmas. She took up the idea and now sells more in that city than she sells in her own.

g. Use Publicity

Publicity is, in essence, free advertising. You can use publicity to draw attention to you, your work, or your company. Publicity can help you become recognized as an "expert" in your field, create good public relations, establish an image, or focus attention on a one-time event.

You can get publicity by using news releases and information pieces that you write yourself and get printed free in trade papers and newspapers. You can write a short article on crafts for the local newspaper or offer yourself for an interview on a local afternoon radio show.

This is actually much easier than you might think. Remember, that to most people busy with shopping, housework, or office jobs, what you are doing is something quite different from the ordinary and bound to arouse interest (see Sample 2).

When writing publicity materials, be as accurate, clear, and brief as possible. While you obviously want to include important information about your work such as its main selling feature (e.g., original wood carvings, winner of the _____ award), the price or range of prices (e.g., from $5 to $50), how to order the product and/or a catalog, remember that this is not an advertisement and if it reads like one, it will probably never be published. The editor who decides whether or not to use your piece is not interested in how well the piece advertises your products, he or she is only interested in whether your piece will entertain the audience. An ad is not news and a price list is not a feature story. Concentrate first on providing the editor and the audience with something interesting that they want to read, and then on promoting you and your work.

For more on using publicity, see *Getting Publicity,* another title in the Self-Counsel Business Series.

SAMPLE 2
NEWS RELEASE

News Release

PILLOW PALS

ROCKINGHORSE CRAFTS LIMITED has just introduced "Pillow Pals," a new line of handcrafted cushions to add to its Doctor Beaver's Friends furry toy animals. The new line features a cat, lamb, elephant, and lion; and more designs are on the way.

The cushions are made from the same high-quality plush that the Rockinghorse people use in their toys and hand puppets. Filled with polyurethane foam chips, these cute furry creatures have two uses. They can double as playmates for your favorite youngster or as a lovely addition to the room of that very special child.

Prices range from $6 to $12 retail. You can order "Pillow Pals" by writing to Rockinghorse Crafts Limited, (*complete address*).

-30-

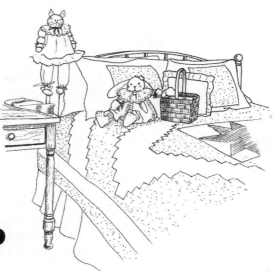

Chapter 9

YOUR WORKSHOP

a. Where to Locate Your Workshop

Let's assume that you have passed the initial start-up phase of your business. You have learned how to make a line of marketable products, you have successfully put your products into stores, and repeat orders are coming in. At this point, you will want to give more thought to the production side of your business, starting perhaps with your workshop.

Perhaps you were fortunate enough to have had an adequate workshop from the beginning and you do not need to create any additional space at this stage. But sooner or later you will find that your growing business requires extra space or at least a reorganization of your existing space. In some cases, say, in a basement workshop, it may be possible to have a larger working space simply by knocking out a partition and making the room bigger. Or perhaps you can expand your operation to the garage as well as the basement. Some craftspeople have even built on additions to their homes to accommodate their craft businesses.

Renting outside space is another option you might want to consider. If you live in a one-bedroom apartment, it may be impossible to expropriate enough space for your business and you will have to

consider buying or renting outside accommodation. There may be a nearby barn or garage that can be converted into a workshop. If you are in a city, you might find an old but still-sturdy building in the downtown area. If you plan to make changes to rented premises, be sure to have an agreement with the owner regarding leasehold improvements.

If at all possible, you should try to operate out of your home, as there are enormous advantages to this. By working at home you save all the time and expense of traveling back and forth between home and workplace. You can avoid making large capital outlays or paying rent for workspace and thereby increase the profits of your business. You can claim a portion of your home expenses, heat, light, and telephone as a tax deduction. You can also more easily employ other members of your family in your business if you want.

If your workshop is located in your home, you will likely be able to operate without any special permission from the local authorities. This is an enormous advantage, especially in the beginning. You don't want bureaucratic hassles while you are trying to establish your business. Most cities and towns have regulations about the kinds of businesses that can be carried out in private residences. Chances are, however, that these will not be too strenuously enforced unless you become a nuisance to a neighbor, in which case the city will have to act. If you are located in the country, interference with neighbors is much less likely to be a problem. (See the section on licenses in chapter 11.)

b. Planning a Workshop

When planning a workshop, whether in your own home or in a separate location, make sure that you will have enough space for your immediate requirements and that it is relatively easy to add more space, should this become necessary in the future.

If you plan to do a lot of retailing from your workshop, you may have to add parking space, unless there is an abundance of street parking in your area. Zoning regulations may have to be considered. A building approved for use as a workshop may not necessarily conform to local regulations if it is used as a retail outlet.

1. The building

If you are constructing a new building, you have a big advantage in that you can plan the layout to suit your exact requirements. Draw up your plans carefully, thinking of things like the location of doors and windows and electrical requirements. Have as many windows as possible on the south side. Make certain that doorways are big enough to accommodate anything you will likely want to bring in or take out of the building.

If you are putting up a new building, you will need permission from the local authorities. Zoning requirements vary greatly from one area to another. The city (or county, if the business is located in an unincorporated area) can give you information concerning the zoning requirements of the area where you plan to locate. Before beginning construction you must apply for a building permit. This usually requires the submission of preliminary sketches of the building for approval and sometimes, at a later stage, complete construction drawings.

If you plan to purchase and renovate an existing building, be sure that your planned use will conform to local regulations. If the building formerly housed an established business, it is possible that the business was set up before the local regulations went into effect. It may be that the owner of such a building is exempt from zoning regulations until he or she applies for a building permit to make structural changes or additions to the building. Always check with the building department before purchasing an existing building for use as a workshop or retail outlet for your crafts.

When building or making major renovations, plan as far ahead as possible for any special requirements you may have. Make certain that there are enough electrical outlets and that they are located where you can use them. Extension cords running all around your workshop are a serious safety hazard and they can get you into trouble with your fire insurance company. Consider also the size and type of electrical service in the building. Is it adequate for the type of equipment you plan to use? If you need three-phase electrical service, check with the power company to be sure that it is available in your area and find out how much extra it costs.

If you put up a new building with its own electrical service, you will probably end up paying commercial rates for electricity, and these are a good deal higher than domestic rates in most areas. If you are operating from your basement or garage and using your home electrical service, there is no reason why you have to pay commercial rates, at least in the beginning.

The same applies to your telephone. There will come a time when you may want a business telephone listing, but with most craft businesses, this will not be necessary in the beginning. If at all possible,

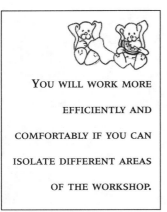

run your electrical equipment from your house and use your home telephone.

When planning your workshop, pay attention to ventilation. Usually an open window is sufficient, but if you are doing certain types of work, such as pottery with an unvented electric kiln, a properly vented electric fan should be installed. If your work creates a lot of dust, you should install hoods or vents over your equipment and have the dust particles or sawdust exhausted to the outside by an electric fan.

If you plan to locate your workshop in a building housing other tenants, you should ensure that your operations do not interfere with them. You don't want complaints about the noise or smells created by your business. Likewise, you won't want to locate your workshop next to a business that creates a lot of noise or dust or one that has heavy vehicles coming and going at all hours of the day.

What about security? If your workshop is located away from your house, it will be vacant at night and on the weekends. Make sure that doors and windows are lockable and that you carry adequate insurance protection. Your coverage should include not only the building itself but tools, equipment, and stock on the premises.

2. The interior

Plan the interior layout of your workshop with the various operations of your craft in mind. You will work more efficiently and comfortably if you can isolate different areas of the workshop. This keeps tools and equipment from getting mixed up and prevents materials from contaminating one another.

When you plan the layout of work benches and tables, think of the flow of work from design to completion. Try to avoid carrying tools and work back and forth any more than necessary. Even in a small, one-person operation, a good layout of tools and working areas in the workshop can make a great difference to the efficiency and profitability of your craft business. If you have employees working for you, efficient organization in the workshop is even more important.

Set aside separate areas for the storage of raw materials and finished goods. This helps immensely when taking inventory and handling orders. Allow plenty of space in the various working areas for the temporary storage of work in progress. If you have to store work at certain stages while you wait for the paint to dry or the material to cool off, think about where you're going to put it so it won't be in your way while you carry on with another part of the operation.

What about a separate area for office or showroom space? If you are pressed for space, a combination of office and showroom area at one end of your workshop is a good idea. Both office and showroom requirements are similar: a clean, quiet place away from the hurly-burly of the workbench where you can show your products to visitors and potential buyers, or eat your lunch.

If you plan to have your office in the same building as your workshop, consider a separate circuit for your computer, especially if you are using equipment like electric motors or kilns, which could cause power surges. You should use a surge protector for your computer in any case, even if it is on a separate circuit, to protect it from power fluctuations originating from sources (i.e., lightning) outside the building. Think about how you will connect your computer to the Internet. If you will be using a dial-up connection, make certain that there is a telephone jack installed in the area where you will have your computer. You should also consider whether to install cable for a high-speed Internet connection. In the event that you should decide to have a high-speed connection later, as more and more people are doing, it is much easier to install the cable at construction time when all parts of the building are accessible.

If you are planning to do a lot of retailing from the workshop, you may want to set aside a separate area. This need not be partitioned off from the working area. In fact, if you are interested in demonstrating your work, it may actually help sales if people can watch you at work. On the other hand, some craftspeople find this a distraction and prefer to keep the selling and production sides of their craft separate. They may want to have a separate shop, partitioned off from the workshop or even have a retail shop in another location.

To sum up: your workshop should be a pleasant and comfortable place in which to work, whether located in your own home or in a separate building. But remember that buildings don't produce profits. They merely provide the working space for you, your tools, and your equipment. They are part of the overhead costs of your business, and your overhead should always be kept as low as possible.

If the needs of your business outgrow your workshop, you can expand to more spacious quarters. If your business is growing, this makes good sense, but wait until your business is ready for it before you take on increased overhead costs. Don't expand too soon and incur large fixed costs that could bankrupt you if business falls off.

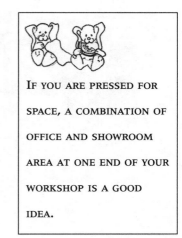

IF YOU ARE PRESSED FOR SPACE, A COMBINATION OF OFFICE AND SHOWROOM AREA AT ONE END OF YOUR WORKSHOP IS A GOOD IDEA.

Chapter 10

PRODUCTION

A s a business person, your goal is to cut costs, increase efficiency, and make as much money as possible. This chapter looks at ways you can do this in the production side of your craft business.

a. Bulk Buying

Whenever possible, you should buy your raw materials in bulk. There are tremendous savings to be realized by the bulk purchase of most items. Of course, buying in bulk requires the outlay of more capital, so it is not recommended until you have got your business off the ground.

As well as buying in bulk, you should try to get as close as possible to the source of your raw materials. In the beginning, you may buy your supplies from a retail craft supply or hobby supply store. In fact, it is not worthwhile trying to "source" all your raw materials at the start of your business. You have other, more important, things to do at this stage.

As soon as your business is off and running, however, you will want to get as close as possible to the manufacturer of your raw materials. This is not always easy. Many wholesalers and distributors are

unwilling to identify their sources of supply, and sometimes manufacturers will only sell their products through a distributor.

Most wholesalers deal in minimum quantities, which are usually more than the quantities you need or can afford to buy in the beginning. To the average wholesaler, your minuscule order may not be worth the trouble. Getting wholesalers to agree to do business with you is sometimes a feat in itself, requiring all the arts of persuasion that you can muster. It usually helps if (without blatant deception) you can somehow implant in the wholesaler's mind the vague notion that someday your company may be a tremendous success and will order huge quantities of their products.

DON'T EXPECT TO GET CREDIT IT IN THE BEGINNING.

It helps also if you agree to pay cash or use a credit card for initial shipments. In most cases, you'll have little choice anyway when you are starting out. Later on, when you have reached the point where your orders are more substantial, you can apply for credit. Don't expect to get it in the beginning.

If you know other craftworkers who use the same material, it may be possible to organize cooperative buying. When you have been in business for some time and get to know other craftworkers in your field, you may find several with whom you could work smoothly in such a cooperative.

The Internet has made it vastly easier to source supplies for just about any kind of business, and crafts are certainly no exception. No matter what material you work with — whether wood, metal, or glass — or what your requirements are — whether it's a part for your bandsaw or a special fastening for your jewelry — you can find information and sources of supply on the Net. You can often do this directly by using a search engine to find what you want. You can also do it indirectly, by finding other craftspeople or organizations on the Net who can supply you with the information you need. Internet bulletin boards and online forums run by craft groups are other places where you can look for suppliers and information on craft techniques.

Your purchasing can be greatly simplified if you design your products with a view to multiple uses of material as much as possible. Besides simplifying purchasing, this helps keep your inventory costs down. If you are ordering material that can be used in only one single item, you will have a problem if sales of that particular item decline. You will be stuck with material that doesn't fit into anything else that you are making.

b. Storage

Buying relatively large quantities of raw materials raises the question of storage. This will be more or less of a problem depending on how bulky your raw materials and finished products are. If you are working in jewelry, storage may not be a major concern, but in woodworking and certain other crafts, storage can be a big problem.

It is no good buying your raw materials in bulk if the savings of bulk buying are offset by the costs of storing your materials until you're ready to use them. You can greatly lower your storage costs and take advantage of bulk buying by using dead storage space. This is simply space outside your studio or workshop where you can store materials for relatively long periods of time. In most cases, this kind of storage will be considerably cheaper than workshop space.

c. Orders

If you do your bookkeeping manually, you need a simple system for keeping track of customer orders to be certain that you ship the right things to the right place at the right time. Without a system, you will have to rely on memory or conduct room-to-room searches of your house and workshop to find a particular order. Shipping the wrong things or shipping an order late can cost you a lot in money and customer goodwill.

Keep your orders in an order book or file them in file folders according to the requested shipping date. This helps you batch shipments together with a similar shipping date and save time by taking a batch of parcels to the post office or having them picked up. It is much easier to plan your production if you can tell at a glance just how much business you have "on the books" (see Sample 3).

If you use computer software with order-entry capability, it is important to make certain that all orders are entered promptly into your system. When you receive an order by mail, over the phone, by fax, or via e-mail, you should enter it into your system as soon as possible. If you sell your products on your own Web site and your site has ordering and transaction capabilities, look into small-business accounting software that allows you to link your online orders directly to your order-entry system.

d. Packing

How you pack your work for shipment to the customer is very important. Even the most beautiful piece of pottery isn't very impressive in several hundred fragments. But breakables aren't the only problem. Many articles require special packing to prevent them from being squashed, scratched, wrinkled, or otherwise damaged in transit.

If you are shipping just a few pieces and these are large or expensive, your packing problems are different from those of someone making production items. Each piece will require its own individually designed container, which in the case of large, fragile items should be a sturdy wooden crate, literally built around the piece.

For most production work, you can use corrugated cardboard cartons. These are available in various degrees of thickness, depending on the nature of the products you are shipping. You will probably have to salvage cartons from your friendly neighborhood supermarket or liquor store in the beginning, but as your business grows, you may want to have your own cartons made with your name stamped on the outside. Obviously, it is cheaper if you can use just one size of carton for all of your products.

When you pack your products, fill in all the spaces left inside the container so that the piece or pieces in the box cannot move around. Depending on what you are packing, crumpled newspaper, excelsior, plastic bubble wrap, or foam rubber will make good packing material. Your cartons should be sealed with strong self-adhesive packing tape, preferably reinforced.

Some carriers have wrapping restrictions. For example, United Parcel Service (UPS) requires that packages be made of corrugated cardboard, with no string or paper on the outside, and sealed with reinforced tape. Check the restrictions of the carrier you plan to use before you take your parcels to the shipping office.

e. Shipping

Mark any special shipping instructions clearly on the outside of your cartons. Glass and other fragile articles should have a wineglass symbol stenciled on each side of the box. Write the address directly on the carton with a waterproof marker or affix a gummed label. Mark your return address prominently on the outside of the carton. Many small-business accounting packages will generate shipping labels from your customer information files. If you don't use a computerized accounting

INSURE ALL SHIPMENTS

NO MATTER HOW YOU

SHIP THEM.

system but have a computer, you can often store customer addresses and generate shipping labels with your word-processing program.

Where possible, follow the customer's instructions as to how goods should be shipped. If this is not possible, ship the cheapest route. In the United States and Canada, most points can be reached by parcel post. Check with your local post office for size and weight restrictions. UPS (United Parcel Service) will accept packages up to 50 pounds in weight and 108 inches length and girth combined. Other options are Fedex (Federal Express) and, in Canada, Purolator.

For fast shipment, most of the major couriers offer airfreight services in the United States and Canada. Many of these promise overnight delivery (though they don't always live up to their promises). They are also fairly expensive and should not be used unless a customer specifically requests it.

Insure all shipments no matter how you ship them. Some services have automatic insurance; UPS, for example, automatically includes insurance up to $100. Where this is insufficient, additional insurance should be purchased. The relatively small extra charge involved is well worth it and can save you a lot of grief if the shipment fails to arrive at its destination.

Most major couriers now offer tracking services, which can be helpful if you want to know when or whether your shipment has arrived safely at its destination. You are provided with a barcode number and a toll-free telephone number that you can call for information on your shipment. Some major couriers also have Web sites on which you can track your shipment by typing in a barcode number.

f. Inventory

1. How to keep track of it

It would be ideal if you had firm orders for all of your work. Some craftspeople do, in fact, produce only on commission, but most production craftworkers find that they have to keep additional supplies of goods on hand at all times. Customers expect you to supply exactly what they want when they want it.

Your inventory consists of your raw materials and work in progress as well as your finished products. Careful management of your inventory can have a major impact on your cash flow, production schedule, and profits. You need an inventory control system or a set of records of everything that goes into or comes out of inventory. This will tell you which of your products is moving well, when you need to reorder supplies, and when to produce in order to have adequate quantities of goods available for filling orders.

If you have a manual accounting system, you can keep this information on index cards, in a looseleaf notebook, or on a columnar pad. It should show additions to and deletions from each particular item that you are keeping track of and have a column showing the current inventory holding of each item (see Sample 3).

Each item in your inventory should have a reorder point. When the quantity is reduced to this reorder point, you produce or reorder that particular item. Experience will soon tell you how fast you use up your materials at a given level of output and how long it takes each of your suppliers to ship materials to you.

If you are choosing a computerized system, you should look carefully at the inventory module of any software package you are considering to see whether it will actually meet your requirements. Many otherwise excellent accounting packages for small businesses are notably weak in the area of inventory management and reporting.

2. How big should your inventory be?

How big an inventory of finished goods should you carry? You must know how fast your finished goods move out of the workshop to your customers. As a rough check on the overall size of your inventory, compare your total inventory with your average monthly sales. Say, for example, you had the following sales for the last half of the year:

July	5,000
Aug.	4,500
Sept.	4,500
Oct.	6,000
Nov.	7,500
Dec.	4,000

Total sales for the six months = 31,500

Average monthly sales = 5,250

COMBINATION ORDER BOOK AND INVENTORY LIST

ORDER BOOK AND INVENTORY LIST FOR "PINECRAFT CO."

ITEM	LG. BOWL RP = 40				SM. BOWL RP = 90				MED. BOWL RP = 50				LG. TRAY RP = 40			
DATE	ORDERS	SHIPPED	MADE	BAL. STOCK	ORDERS	SHIPPED	MADE	BAL. STOCK	ORDERS	SHIPPED	MADE	BAL. STOCK	ORDERS	SHIPPED	MADE	BAL. STOCK
JUNE 2	20			50	35		40	90	30			29				45
JUNE 3		5		45	20	15		75	20	10	60	79	8	8		37
JUNE 4	25				40		50	125				79		10		27
JUNE 5	20	5		40	10	30		95	25	55	35	59				

RP = REORDER POINT (at this point more of each item would be reordered or made)
ORDERS = All orders on hand for this item
SHIPPED = Number of items shipped — inventory deletions
MADE = Number of items made — inventory additions
BAL. STOCK = Number of items currently in inventory

Your inventory at the end of December is 7,800. Since you have found that a total inventory of about 30 days average sales is sufficient for normal operation and you know that the two months following December are your slack season, you could reduce your inventory to around 5,250 and still have plenty of stock on hand to fill orders.

If you are working with an assistant or one or more employees, you will probably want to reduce your inventory in order to keep your costs down. However, if you are running your craft business single-handedly, you may want to allow your inventory to remain a little higher than the above formula would suggest.

The reason for this is as follows. You will most likely find that there are fairly pronounced seasonal fluctuations in your sales. The pre-Christmas buying season may be one of your busiest times or the spring months may be your peak sales period. If you are running a single-person operation, you will spend a lot of your time selling, shipping, and invoicing in the peak periods and you will not be able to do as much production. You must therefore build up your inventory in anticipation of these busy sales periods.

YOU MUST BUILD UP YOUR INVENTORY IN ANTICIPATION OF BUSY SALES PERIODS.

3. How much of each item should you carry?

Apart from the overall size of your finished-goods inventory, there is the question of just how much of each particular item you should carry. Even if you are making a single product, there are likely to be several different styles and sizes. More likely you will have a variety of different items. How much of each particular item should you carry in inventory?

If you break down your inventory and sales figures as in Table 2, you may find that one or two items account for a relatively large proportion of your sales.

From this you can see that items A and B should receive the most attention, as they account for 70 percent of your sales. You can reduce your inventory of items E, F, and G, as they are relatively unimportant to your total sales picture.

Even though you are close enough to your business to know which items are your best movers, it is worthwhile to do this little analysis for verification. No matter how small your business, you want to plan your production so that you concentrate your efforts on those products that are selling best.

TABLE 2
INVENTORY/SALES BREAKDOWN

Products	Percent inventory	Percent of sales
A, B	30	70
C, D	30	20
E, F, G	40	10

Many large companies now use automated systems that link inventory management with other areas of their operations, allowing them, for example, to schedule "just in time" delivery of their raw materials in order to keep their inventory costs as low as possible. For most craft businesses, these systems are currently too elaborate and too expensive to be of much use. But new small-business software is being developed all the time, and in the near future even small businesses may be able to automate most of the information management aspects of their operations.

Chapter 11

RULES AND REGULATIONS

This chapter contains vital information that you as a professional craftsperson or operator of a craft business must know. It is here rather than at the beginning of the book for a very good reason. If you started off by reading this chapter first, you might have felt that there are so many complex government rules and regulations that you would be better off not going into business.

Government in its wisdom has decreed that, as a business person, you are automatically appointed to the job of a tax collector (whether you like it or not). Government has also created a vast body of legislation telling you, the independent business person, what you must and must not do. Many of these rules and regulations apply to you only if you become an employer or if you have separate business premises. If you are working at home and have no employees, most of them will not affect you.

No matter what kind of craft business you operate, however, you should read this chapter through carefully to determine which regulations apply to you. If you have any doubts about the application of a particular law or regulation, you should write to the government department or agency concerned and request clarification.

The following sections apply to both the United States and Canada. Where there are significant differences between the two countries, as in the case of payroll taxes, they are treated separately.

Regulations affecting craft businesses in Canada and the United States vary from state to state and from province to province. In some cases, as with licensing and zoning laws for example, they are different for each town, county, or municipality. Moreover, laws and regulations are subject to constant and sometimes bewildering change.

In a book of this size and scope, it is not possible to cover all the rules and regulations in all the many different jurisdictions. I have adopted the approach of outlining the main areas of concern to most craftspeople. In this way, the individual craftsperson should be in a position to decide if, when, and how much additional information (from more specialized publications and/or the regulatory agencies themselves) or outside assistance (such as professional legal or accounting advice) he or she needs.

a. Retail Sales Tax

Most states and provinces charge a retail sales tax. This tax is levied on all sales directly to the consumer. If you are selling your work directly to the consumer and you are in a jurisdiction that has this kind of tax, you are responsible for collecting it and remitting it to the government at regular intervals. You are required to apply for a sales tax number from the department of revenue or finance. They will issue you a certificate of authority to collect the tax, send you reporting forms and all necessary instructions, and advise you of dates (usually monthly) for remitting tax collected.

If you have a state or provincial retail sales tax permit, you do not have to pay retail sales tax on materials bought for use in products you plan to resell. Some merchants may want you to fill out a form of declaration stating that the goods purchased are intended for use as a component part in an article for resale, but most will be content to have your state or provincial retail sales tax number.

b. Goods and Services Tax (Canada)

The goods and services tax (GST) is a federal sales tax applied at every level of the economy (manufacture, wholesale, retail) at which goods and services are exchanged. (A very small number of goods and services are exempt.) All companies and individuals carrying on business in Canada have to register for and collect the GST. A business must charge its customers the GST on all sales and must pay the GST on all business purchases. If the amount of GST a business charges is more than the amount paid, the difference is owed to the government. If the amount paid out is larger than the amount charged, a business is entitled to a refund of the difference. The accounting period for the GST varies from annual to monthly, depending on the size of a business.

The only relief for the small craft business operator is the provision that businesses with gross annual sales of less than $30,000 are not required to register for or to collect the GST. However, there is a catch: businesses that choose not to register will have to pay the GST on all their purchases, and will not be entitled to refunds.

If you have any questions about the GST or how it applies to your particular product, contact Canada Revenue Agency (Business Enquiries) at 1-800-959-2221 and ask them to send you the *Guide for Canadian Small Businesses*. This publication can also be downloaded on the Internet at <www.cra-arc.gc.ca/E/pub/tg/rc4070/rc4070-e.pdf>.

Note: In the Atlantic provinces, the federal and provincial governments implemented a harmonized sales tax, blending the GST with the provincial sales tax. Contact your local tax office for details.

c. Payroll Taxes

The United States Internal Revenue Service (IRS) and Revenue Canada define an employee in similar terms. According to the IRS:

> *Everyone who performs services subject to the will and control of an employer both as to what shall be done and how it shall be done, is an employee. It does not matter that the employer permits the employee considerable discretion and freedom of action, if the employer has the legal right to control both the method and the result of the services. Though not always applicable, some of the characteristics of the term "employee" are that the employer has the right to discharge him and furnishes him with tools and a place to work.*

If you have employees, you have to collect taxes from them. For governments, taxation at source is the best thing that was ever invented. For employers, it means that you spend a lot of your time as an unpaid tax collector. Payroll taxes are the main reason why hiring people to work for you will just about double your paperwork.

After reading this section, you may well decide that you don't want to become an employer. In chapter 16, the section on cottage industries discusses how to get work done for you without hiring employees.

1. If you are in the United States

To meet your legal obligations as an employer, you should write to the federal and state tax departments at least one month before hiring your first employee.

(a) Federal requirements

You can call the IRS at 1-800-829-1040 and ask for the Small Business Tax Kit #454. Tax information for starting a business can be found by going to <www.irs.gov/businesses/small/index.html>. For a Federal Tax ID number, contact the Internal Revenue Service and ask for Form SS4. This Form is available through their Web site at <https://sa.www4 .irs.gov/sa_vign/newFormSS4.do>.

The amount of income tax that you must withhold from each employee's paycheck is determined by using the withholding tables. You are also obliged to withhold the social security tax or Federal Insurance Contributions Act (FICA) tax. This must be matched by an equal amount from you as an employer.

These amounts must be remitted by you on the federal payroll tax return, a special form which you will receive compliments of the IRS. Remittance due dates depend on the amounts collected; they may be due quarterly or in some instances may be due as soon as three banking days after the end of the payroll period. Remittances may be made to an authorized commercial bank or a federal reserve bank.

The FICA tax is not payable for an individual employed by his or her spouse or for a child under the age of 21 employed by a parent.

As an employer, you are also liable for the federal unemployment tax. This is a tax imposed on you, the employer; you do not deduct it from your employee's wages. This tax applies if you paid wages of more than $1,500 in a calendar quarter in the current or preceding calendar year. An annual return is filed on a special form which will be sent to you.

For more detailed information, consult *The Small Business Resource Guide,* which can be ordered from:

National Technical Information Service
5285 Port Royal Road
Springfield, VA 22161
1-877-CDFORMS
1-877-233-6767

Or you can order a free copy of this publication on CD-ROM by going to <www.irs.gov/businesses/small/article/0,,id=98229,00.html>.

(b) State requirements

Most states have an income tax on wages and require employers to withhold state income tax. Most states also have employer-paid state unemployment insurance. You will need to contact the Department of Revenue for state taxes (if any). Consult your local telephone directory in the State Government section for the office in your state. Many states require employers to have workers' compensation insurance. This provides wage, disability, and death benefits to employees hurt or killed on the job. Some states have their own insurance plans, others require that you obtain coverage with a private insurance company.

2. If you are in Canada

You should contact the Canada Revenue Agency at least one month before becoming an employer and request an employer's tax number, tax guide, and tables for the amounts to be withheld from employees' pay. Income tax, Canada Pension Plan contributions, and employment insurance premiums must be deducted from each employee's paycheck in accordance with sets of tables, which Canada Revenue Agency will send to you.

As an employer, you are required to contribute an employer's portion to both the pension plan and unemployment insurance plan. Pension plan deductions from employees must also be matched by an equal amount from you. Unemployment deductions must be accompanied by an amount that is (at time of writing) 1.4 times the amount deducted from the employee.

The amounts deducted from employees, together with employer contributions, must be remitted to Canada Revenue Agency accompanied by a special form that they will send you. Remittances are due

IGNORANCE OF THE LAW IS NOT LEGAL GROUNDS FOR NONCOMPLIANCE.

on the fifteenth of the following month and may be made at any branch of a chartered bank or by mail.

Workers' compensation is usually provided by a provincial workers' compensation board. If you have employees, you will be assessed on the basis of the size of your payroll according to a rate scale that is based on industry statistics. Unfortunately, this can be unfair to a small craft operation, since most craft businesses don't correspond to standard industry classifications. For example, a small woodworking shop making handcrafted furniture may be assessed on the basis of rates for the furniture industry.

d. Deadlines for Government Remittances

Whether you operate in the United States or in Canada, you should be aware that deadlines for sales taxes and payroll taxes are rigorously enforced. If a remittance is due on or by the fifteenth of the month, for example, it must be paid on or by the fifteenth. If you are even one day late, you are subject to automatic fines.

Also, in both countries you are presumed to know the law. As horrifying as this may seem, ignorance of the law is not legal grounds for noncompliance. Whenever you are in doubt about whether a particular statute applies to your business, contact the department or agency concerned and get the full facts.

e. Licenses

Most towns, municipalities, and counties in the United States and Canada require businesses to have a local business license. This can cost anywhere from $10 to $200 and is usually renewed annually. But a license will rarely be necessary if you operate a small craft business out of your home. Discretion and prudence are the key words here. If you are quietly producing handmade widgets in your basement, no one will likely bother you, but if you expand the retail side of your operation to the point where you have signs prominently displayed and a lot of customers coming and going, you are likely to attract the attention of the local authorities, who may require you to hold a license.

If you have a separate workshop building or retail outlet, you will be subject to all the licensing requirements, zoning laws, building regulations, and health and fire codes. You will also be subject to local taxes on real estate, water consumption, and business premises. Real estate taxes are based on the assessed real value of your property. Business taxes are usually applied directly against the tenant or business operator. Business taxes may be based on the property assessment, the annual rental value, the value of year-end inventory or another basis.

It is impossible to detail the requirements of all local governments. Any or all of the above local taxes and regulations might apply to you. If you have separate business premises, the safest bet is to contact your local authority before opening your doors for business. Also, wherever possible, operate your business out of your own home, at least in the beginning. Later on, when things are off and running, you may need separate premises and you can tackle the local bureaucracy then.

f. Labeling

Depending on what you make, there are certain labeling requirements you should be aware of.

1. In the United States

All packages and labels on goods must conform to the Federal Fair Packaging and Labeling Act. This requires that a label identify the product, give the name of the manufacturer or distributor, and show the net quantity of the contents. You can get a copy of the act from the Federal Trade Commission, Washington, DC, 20580.

Textiles, fabrics, and clothing must be labeled in accordance with the Textile Fiber Products Identification Act and Federal Trade Commission Act regarding the care labeling of wearing apparel. Essentially, the first of these laws requires that textile, fabric, and clothing labels state the fiber content or composition of the fabric, the name of the manufacturer or distributor, and the country of origin if the goods are imported. The second piece of legislation requires that labels on finished wearing apparel or piece goods intended to be made into wearing apparel "clearly disclose instructions for the care and maintenance of such goods" (e.g., lukewarm wash). The Federal Trade Commission will supply you with copies of these laws.

A few states require that upholstered or stuffed articles have labels identifying the stuffing material.

2. In Canada

In Canada, prepackaged products must have a label identifying the product, the manufacturer or distributor, and showing the net quantity (where applicable). The quantity must be in metric units and the information must be printed in both English and French.

Textiles, fabrics, and wearing apparel must be labeled with the fiber content or composition of the fabric according to the Textiles Labelling Act. There are other regulations governing the sale of consumer textile fabric products. For detailed information, contact:

Industry Canada
235 Queen Street
Ottawa, ON K1A 0H5
Tel.: (613) 954-2788
Fax: (613) 954-1894

Some Canadian provinces require the makers of stuffed articles to be licensed and to label all products with the type of stuffing used and whether it is new or used material. Fortunately, the provinces that have these requirements will accept the label authorized by the province of Ontario. To apply for an Ontario license, contact:

Government of Ontario
General Inquiry Unit
250 Yonge Street
Toronto, ON M5B 2N5
Tel: (416) 326-8555
1-800-268-1142

g. Contracts

If you are engaged in production crafts, selling your work is fairly straightforward, involving simply a sales slip or invoice. It is advisable to get a signed purchase order, particularly for a new account. If the order is a large one, you should insist on a signed purchase order before proceeding with the work. A contract should be signed if goods are ordered to a customer's particular specifications.

If you are producing one-of-a-kind pieces, you will probably use contracts more often than someone in production crafts. If you produce a unique piece of work for a particular customer, it may be unsalable elsewhere and involve a considerable amount of your time and raw materials. To protect yourself, some kind of written contract is mandatory.

In the United States, there are certain situations where the law requires a contract to be in writing. The Statute of Frauds, in effect in most states, requires any agreement that cannot be completed within one year to be in writing. If, for example, you are commissioned to produce a wall hanging to be installed in the foyer of a new building to be completed in 18 months, the agreement must be in writing to be legally valid.

If you are making relatively expensive one-of-a-kind pieces in the United States, you may also be affected by the Uniform Commercial Code. This statute, which is in effect in most states, requires a written contract whenever goods over $500 in value are sold.

A contract can be anything from a simple verbal agreement to a 20-page legal document. Essentially, it should cover what is to be produced, the cost, method of payment, and completion date, and it should provide methods for resolving any possible problems that could arise in the course of the transaction.

A CONTRACT CAN BE ANYTHING FROM A SIMPLE VERBAL AGREEMENT TO A 20-PAGE LEGAL DOCUMENT.

1. Contracts with retail clients

If you sell a unique piece directly to a client, you should consider a simple written agreement covering the following:

- Date of sale, name of purchaser, description of the work, price

- Terms of payment. In the case of a work that involves a substantial commitment in time or raw materials, you should structure the contract so that you receive several progress payments. A useful arrangement would be for you to receive a design fee when the agreement is signed, a second progress payment upon completion of a distinct phase of the work, and final payment upon completion of the whole work.

- Whether you want to reserve reproduction rights

2. Consignment contracts

If you place a work with a shop or gallery on consignment, you should include the following in your agreement:

- The selling price and how it is to be set

- The percentage to be paid to you (while this should be in the range of 70 percent to 75 percent when dealing with craft shops, some of the more prestigious galleries will give you less, perhaps as little as 50 percent in the case of unique one-of-a-kind pieces)

- Whether the shop or gallery has exclusive rights and, if so, in what area

- Whether the shop or gallery receives any commissions on direct sales by the artist/craftsperson

- Who is responsible for insurance while the work is on exhibit

- The duration of the agreement

h. Income Taxes

Laws governing income tax for businesses and individuals are extremely complex. Moreover, they are subject to constant changes and in some cases even to different interpretations. You are advised to seek the assistance of a competent professional to help you with your business income taxes.

Chapter 12

GETTING HELP

a. Getting a Loan from a Financial Institution

If you are fortunate, your craft business will be able to generate sufficient cash to meet its operating requirements and you won't need to borrow money. The cost of borrowing is an extra business expense, and the fewer expenses you have, the better.

However, many successful craft businesses from time to time need extra cash. It may be that your sales have expanded rapidly and you need an operating loan for a relatively short period of time. Or perhaps you are putting up a new workshop and require long-term financing.

Where you go for financial help depends on whether you are in the United States or Canada. The u.s. banking system is much more responsive to the needs of small enterprises than is the banking system in Canada. If your business is in Canada, you are much more likely to go to some government agency for a loan. This difference aside, loan application procedures are similar in both countries.

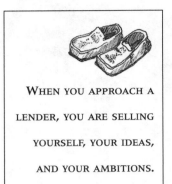

1. Select the right financial institution

The first step is to select the financial institution that you are going to approach. The best bet is to select an institution where you already have a history of responsible financial dealings. If you don't have an existing relationship with an institution, you may want to shop around a bit to find one that suits you in terms of location or how approachable the manager appears.

2. Be well prepared

Always be well prepared when you approach a potential lender. You will feel more confident and the lender is more likely to be impressed by your organization if you have a good, computer-generated presentation.

Present the lender with a statement of your cash flow (see chapter 14 on preparing a cash flow statement) and explain precisely how much money you want to borrow and why. Be precise and very specific. Show how your business can be expected to generate the cash to repay the loan.

Be prepared to provide financial statements (profit and loss statements and balance sheets) for the last three years of operation of your business. If you have been in business for a shorter period of time, you should bring all your existing financial statements.

If you are borrowing money to get your business started, you won't have past financial records so you should put increased emphasis on the future projections for your business.

3. Sell yourself

When you approach a lender, you are selling yourself, your ideas, and your ambitions. If you want to win his or her confidence, you must be prepared to answer all questions as candidly as possible. Bring a personal resume that includes your general and educational background. Provide details of your personal financial situation: how much personal debt you have and what assets you own.

4. Security

The question of security for your loan will inevitably arise. You can be sure that you will not get a loan unless you have some tangible assets as security. Your strategy should be to sell the lender on your business plans and their soundness before discussing what security you can give. If you own your home and are willing to mortgage it, or mortgage it further if you are currently making mortgage payments, a lender is likely to lend you money on it.

When you borrow money for your business, you are personally liable to pay it back. If your company is incorporated, the lender will require a personal guarantee from you. Your financial institution may also require you to sign an assignment of receivables declaration, which gives it legal authority to step in and collect any money owed to you by your customers if your business goes under. You may also have to sign a postponement of claim declaration, which, in effect, gives the financial institution priority over all other creditors of your company in bankruptcy proceedings.

If they agree to grant you a loan, financial institutions will usually require you to take out property and liability insurance on your business and a life insurance policy on yourself, naming the bank as beneficiary.

5.   What if they turn you down?

A financial institution may come up with a variety of reasons for turning down your request for a loan. If you don't succeed at the first lender you try, go to others. There are plenty of institutions around. It's a little easier in the United States than in Canada because the U.S. banking system is more competitive.

If you shop around and still can't get a loan, don't give up. There is a chance that the government may lend you the money for your business.

b. Getting a Loan from the Government

Preparing your case for a government loan or loan guarantee is not all that different from applying for a loan from a financial institution. You must provide the fullest possible documentation — cash flow statement, financial statements, personal resume — and be prepared to answer a lot of questions. You must also be prepared to provide collateral or security for your loan.

1.   In the United States

Although some states have loan programs, the most promising government source of financial help for the small craft business is the

United States Small Business Administration or SBA. The SBA has a loan guarantee program whereby a commercial bank loans you money and the SBA guarantees a substantial part (up to 85 percent) of the loan. Direct SBA loans are available under a program for "economically and socially disadvantaged" businesses.

In order to qualify for an SBA loan or loan guarantee, a business must be unable to obtain financing from the private sector. In other words, you must be turned down by the banks before the SBA will lend you any money. The SBA makes or guarantees a relatively small number of loans a year and competition for the available funds is fairly keen. SBA loans also involve a lot of red tape, completing of forms, and adherence to a set of operating guidelines that can limit your freedom and flexibility. For more information contact the Small Business Administration at:

SBA Answer Desk
6302 Fairview Rd., Suite 300
Charlotte, North Carolina 28210
1-800-UASK-SBA (1-800-827-5722)
E-mail: answerdesk@sba.gov

The SBA provides a variety of services to small businesses. You can find out more about these services by visiting their Web site at <www.sba.gov>.

2. In Canada

Canada has a number of federal and provincial agencies that lend money to businesses, large and small.

At the federal level, the most promising source for a small craft business is the Business Development Bank of Canada (BDC). The BDC usually lends money under a number of programs suited to small- and medium-sized businesses. The offices of the BDC can also give advice on a variety of other options for borrowing money from the government.

Many Canadian provinces have set up provincial Crown corporations that make loans to businesses. Contact your provincial department of development or commerce for details.

c. Other Government Assistance

In addition to loans and loan guarantees, other forms of aid may be available from governments. Government aid programs are complicated by the fact that some governments regard crafts as an educational or cultural field, while others see them primarily as an economic activity.

1. In the United States

The federal government provides financial assistance through the National Endowment for the Arts. These funds are not available directly to individuals but must be applied for through an arts or crafts organization. This type of assistance is more applicable to the artist/craftsperson or person producing one-of-a-kind pieces. For details, contact your state arts or crafts organization or the American Craft Council (see Appendix 2).

State assistance for small business varies from state to state; it is impossible to generalize for all 50 states. Some states, such as Connecticut, Massachusetts, and New Jersey, have extensive programs for helping small business. Others, such as Delaware and Idaho, have few programs. Contact your state economic development agency for details on the programs available in your state. (See Appendix 1 for a directory of local, state, and provincial development agencies.)

2. In Canada

There is much more government assistance available to a crafts business in Canada than in the United States. At the federal level, artists and craftspeople are eligible for direct grants from the Canada Council under a variety of different programs. Small craft businesses can receive financial assistance toward the cost of new buildings and equipment from Industry Canada.

There are many other federal assistance programs available. Many of them are applicable to a small craft business. The best way to find out about these programs is to ask your local office of the Business Development Bank of Canada. The BDC also has information to help you if you are a U.S. citizen who wishes to set up a business in Canada.

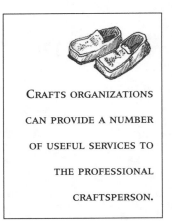

CRAFTS ORGANIZATIONS CAN PROVIDE A NUMBER OF USEFUL SERVICES TO THE PROFESSIONAL CRAFTSPERSON.

At the provincial level, a wide variety of aid programs are available to small businesses. These include loans, loan guarantees, outright grants for the purchase of new buildings and equipment, training programs for new employees, and marketing assistance programs. Some provinces, such as Nova Scotia, have financial assistance programs that will pay a portion of the costs of attending out-of-province trade shows and other marketing costs. To find out about these programs, write to your provincial department of industry or development.

d. Crafts Organizations

Crafts organizations can provide a number of useful services to the professional craftsperson. (See Appendix 2 for a list of national, provincial, and state craft organizations in the U.S.A. and Canada.)

1. Marketing

Many crafts organizations run one or more retail fairs a year. Some provide wholesale opportunities for their members in the form of a register of producers that can be consulted by store owners. A few run craft fairs for wholesale buyers, and some organizations put on marketing seminars.

2. Other services

Some crafts organizations provide group insurance policies for their members. An organization may be able to offer assistance in the form of a loan or application for a grant for an individual craftsperson. National, state, and provincial crafts organizations can lobby governments on behalf of craftspeople. There is a great need for this in the area of government procurement policies (such as the purchase of crafts for public buildings).

Crafts organizations can also help in the dissemination of information among craftspeople. Many organizations publish a newsletter or magazine and can provide lists of craft courses and suppliers of craft materials and craft books. More and more craft organizations are setting up Web sites where they provide a variety of informational services to the craft community, members and non-members alike. Some organizations also organize seminars and put on workshops on particular crafts (e.g., weaving, metalworking, pottery).

3. Should you join a crafts organization?

There are a variety of reasons for joining a craft organization. Perhaps you simply want to participate in the craft shows put on by the organization. You may want to serve on one of the committees. Perhaps you just want to meet other craftspeople and exchange ideas about making or selling your products.

Many craft organizations aim to serve the interests of both production and designer craftspeople and have memberships reflecting both types; other organizations are oriented towards one of production or designer crafts. Many organizations also have significant numbers of members who are involved with crafts part-time or in ways that have nothing to do with making a living (i.e., teachers at art or craft schools). Generally, the more diverse the organization the better. Part-time craftspeople often go on to become full-time, and many craftspeople make both production and one-of-a-kind pieces. Apart from specific benefits, such as participating in crafts shows, the opportunities provided by crafts organizations to meet and network with other craftspeople can be invaluable.

KEEPING FINANCIAL RECORDS

a. What Kind of System?

Bookkeeping. Ugh! That is the reaction of most craftspeople to the record-keeping side of their business. Keeping records is seen as an unpleasant distraction to the main business of making and selling their work. Most craftworkers would rather spend their time at the loom or the wheel than in the office.

While it may never become a joy to do, bookkeeping can be made more pleasant (or less unpleasant) by having a good system that you can readily understand. Moreover, a good bookkeeping system can be vital to the success of your business, letting you know at all times just how much money you are making.

There are two basic reasons for keeping accurate and up-to-date accounts. Whether you like it or not, the tax department insists that you supply it with certain information at regular intervals along with a slice of the business profits. Keeping adequate records is not only necessary to comply with the law but to ensure that you do not pay one single penny more in taxes than you have to.

A good bookkeeping system should tell you your exact financial position at all times. This will allow you to determine just how much

money you are making and where your business is going. If you're heading for trouble, a good system will enable you to spot problems early and take corrective action before it is too late. Accurate records are also essential if your business needs to borrow money, either for normal operating requirements or to finance expansion.

Do you need the services of a professional accountant? The answer to this should be no, at least in the beginning stages. Once your business is off and running, you will need an accountant about once a year, chiefly to advise you on your tax return, especially if your business is incorporated. But remember that first your business has to make money. If it doesn't, then you won't need books or an accountant at all. In the beginning, stay away from professional accountants who work out of large regional or national firms. Most of them know next to nothing about running a small business like yours, and they may charge you enormous fees for advice of little practical value.

What you need is a set of records that you can understand and maintain yourself. You may need help from an accountant in setting it up and you would certainly be wise to have an accountant review your year-end tax return. However, it will save you a lot of money if you can handle your own routine bookkeeping chores, at least in the beginning stages of your business. Later on, when your business is making a lot of money, you can make your record-keeping system as sophisticated as you want.

The basic components of a simple manual bookkeeping system for a small craft business start-up are outlined in this chapter. Computerized accounting systems are included in the discussion for those who are past the start-up stage. As your business grows, you may begin to find manual accounting too cumbersome, yet you may not feel the situation really requires a computerized system, either. At this point, you may contemplate getting a "one-write" system. This is a method that uses carbonized paper to post your sales automatically to a sales journal and ledger card. This can save effort, but most one-write systems are fairly expensive and much less versatile than computerized systems. You may be better off waiting until your business reaches the point where you are ready for computerized accounting.

Accountants and small business consultants used to have a kind of rule of thumb for deciding the point at which a small business

WHAT YOU NEED IS A SET OF RECORDS THAT YOU CAN UNDERSTAND AND MAINTAIN YOURSELF.

could efficiently adopt a computerized accounting system. They would look at sales volume or number of client accounts or employees. Nowadays, most of these rules have gone out the window. Improvements in accounting software mean that even very small businesses with no employees and only a small number of clients can now efficiently use computerized accounting programs.

There are literally hundreds of accounting packages on the market. Picking the right one is critical; a mistake here can mean frustration and a lot of wasted time. Fortunately, there are a number of steps you can take beforehand to make certain that the package you choose is the right one for you.

Having a simple manual accounting system already in place makes the process much easier because you will already know most of the things you want your accounting system to do. Most computerized systems will do a lot more. In fact, one of the most common mistakes made is to pick a system with all kinds of wonderful features that you don't want or need, but without the essential features that you really do need.

For this reason, you should first draw up a list of just what you need your system to do, paying particular attention to any special needs of your business. For example, you might need to keep track of work put out to stores on consignment, or payments to piece workers (independent contractors who produce work for you in their own homes). Perhaps you'll require the ability to generate invoices in a language other than English. Think also of additional features that you might like your system to have, such as inventory tracking.

Once you have determined what you want your system to do right now, you should then think of what you might want it to do in the future. If, for example, you are thinking of doing your business banking online at some point, you might want your system to have the capability to deposit and withdraw money from your financial institution. Planning for future needs allows you to more easily expand your system when the time comes.

Armed with a checklist of your requirements, you can narrow your search to software packages designed to suit the needs of businesses like yours. You can ask other craft business owners what they use or read reviews in small-business periodicals or craft magazines like *The Crafts Report*.

Needless to say, you want to be certain your computer has sufficient power and hard drive capacity to handle your accounting software. If you bought your computer within the last two or three years, you will most likely have more than enough computing power (RAM) and hard-drive memory for just about any small-business accounting package you will want to consider. But if you have an older computer, it is a good idea to check carefully before you commit yourself to new accounting software.

You can often obtain evaluation copies of small-business accounting packages or, by visiting the Web sites of software vendors, you can see demonstrations of how the software actually works. It's worthwhile taking the time to do this. As well as meeting your present and immediate future accounting requirements, any package you are considering should be easy to set up and use. The package you choose should offer all the main components needed for a complete accounting system. The main components are —

- accounts payable,
- accounts receivable,
- general ledger,
- inventory,
- job costing,
- order entry,
- payroll, and
- system manager.

The three most widely used small business accounting programs currently on the market are —

- Simply Accounting by AccPac (www.accpac.com),
- QuickBooks Pro by Intuit (www.quickbooks.com), and
- One Write Plus by Peachtree Division of Sage Software (www.peachtree.com).

You should not, however, limit yourself to a consideration of only these three. The most important factor is that any system you choose fit your specific business requirements; don't choose a package based on its general popularity, price, or number of advanced features.

b. The Essentials of a Good Bookkeeping System

Whether your accounting system is manual, one-write, or computerized, maintaining a good, inexpensive set of records for a craft business involves three elements:

(i) Do as much of the basic bookkeeping work as possible yourself. It is a waste of money to ask your accountant to total invoices or to make journal entries for you. If you are doing your accounting manually and your business grows to the point where you can't handle these chores, then consider handing them over to your spouse, a part-time bookkeeper, or a computer.

(ii) Hand over the "higher-level" accounting functions and tax matters to your accountant. You should let your accountant show you how to set up and maintain your general ledger and either complete or review your year-end financial statements and income tax return.

(iii) Always be up to date in your record keeping. Never allow yourself to get so far behind that you are faced with a mountain of backlogged work and the task appears hopeless. Much of the onerous nature of bookkeeping work can be relieved if things are kept up to date. More important, not being up to date can mean that your records are not much use to you. During a critical phase of your business you will have to make decisions based on the latest information. Four- or five-month-old data may not be of much use to you.

You should retain your bookkeeping records in your possession except when your accountant is actually working on them. This applies especially to your general ledger. This is one of your most valuable business tools; it should be up to date and accessible to you at all times. You should not have to call up your accountant to access the information in your general ledger.

c. Income

You need to keep a record of all money received and, if you grant credit, a record of all money owing to you. When you sell your work at retail, either at craft markets or in your own store, make out a sales slip, and be sure to keep a copy for yourself. Alternatively, you may enter the figures neatly in a ruled notebook. In either case, be sure to collect and separately record the sales tax.

1. Invoices and order forms

When you sell to shops, you should complete an invoice showing the customer's name and address, purchase order number, date of purchase, description and cost of goods, and any other charges, such as freight. Make sure that your terms of payment are stated clearly on the invoice form. If you use a manual bookkeeping system, you can buy blank invoice forms in triplicate and rubber stamp them with your name, address, and terms of sale (see Sample 4); however, it looks more professional if you have your forms printed.

If you have a computer, you can often use your spreadsheet software to prepare invoices. Microsoft Excel, for example, has built-in templates that allow you to fill out, store, and print invoices. With a good accounting program, you should be able to generate invoices easily. With a dot matrix printer you can use triplicate forms; with an ordinary ink-jet printer you can print three copies. However you do it, you need at least three copies of the invoice. (If you export your product to certain countries, you could need five or even more copies.) Send the original to the customer by mail under separate cover, send one copy as a packing slip with the goods, and keep one copy for your records. Invoices should be numbered consecutively, and your copies should be filed numerically so that they are easy to retrieve. Even if you have a computerized system, you should retain a set of printed copies for your records.

2. Managing accounts receivable

If you sell all your work for cash, you don't need to read the rest of this section. Chances are, however, that some of your sales to stores will be charge sales, so you will need some way of collecting from your customers.

At the end of the month, each customer should receive a statement of his or her account showing the outstanding balance. The easiest way to do this in a manual system is to head up a ledger sheet for each customer, including the customer's address and credit limit. On this sheet, record all invoices and payments together with their respective dates for that particular customer. These sheets have holes punched in them so that they can be bound together in alphabetical order — this is called your accounts receivable ledger (see Sample 5).

PLAIN RUBBER STAMPED INVOICE

1034

ROCKINGHORSE CRAFTS LIMITED
Tantallon R.R. 2, Site 4, Box 7, N.S. B0J 3J0
Tel. (902) 835-5287 or 826-2272

SOLD TO

ABC Craft Shop
123 Main St.
Anytown, N.Y.

SHIP TO

DATE	SHIPPED VIA	FED. LICENCE NO.	PROV. LICENCE NO.	YOUR ORDER NO.	OUR ORDER NO.	TERMS	SALESMAN
May 25	UPS			1207	102	NET 30	

QUANTITY	DESCRIPTION	UNIT PRICE	AMOUNT
6	LG. BEAVER	9.50	57.00
12	SM. BEAVER	6.50	78.00
4	LG. SAINT BERNARD	47.50	190.00
12	BEAVER HAND PUPPET	8.00	96.00
	SUBTOTAL		421.00
	FREIGHT		21.50
	TOTAL		442.50

6 PKG. Shipped May 25

MOORE BUSINESS FORMS   3   7060E   MOORE BUSINESS FORMS 7S649E

E & OE

INVOICE

SAMPLE 5
ACCOUNTS RECEIVABLE LEDGER

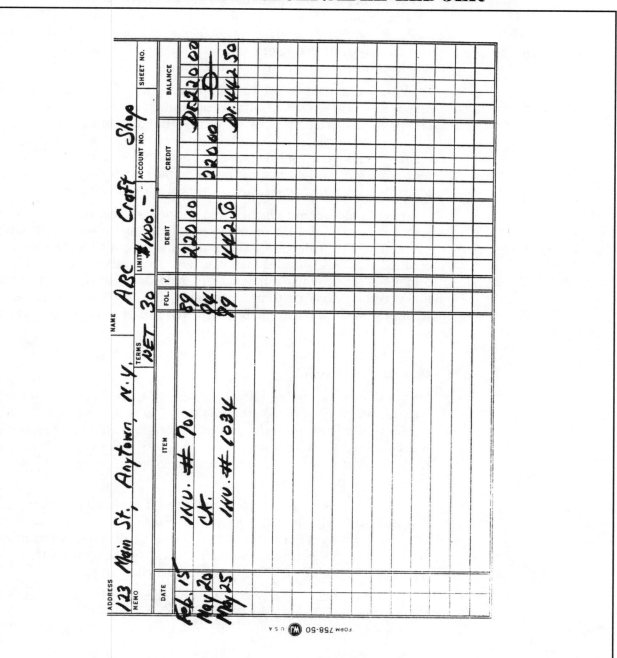

DATE	ITEM	FOL.	✓	DEBIT	CREDIT	BALANCE
Feb. 15	INV. # 701	89		220 00		Dr 220 00
May 20	Ck.	04			220 00	O
May 25	INV. # 1034	99		442 50		Dr. 442 50

ADDRESS: 123 Main St., Anytown, N.Y.

NAME: ABC Craft Shop

MEMO

TERMS: NET 30

LIMIT: $1000.—

ACCOUNT NO.

SHEET NO.

FORM 758-50 Ⓦ U.S.A.

KEEP A DETAILED RECORD OF ALL YOUR EXPENSES AS THEY OCCUR.

A computerized system will save you a lot of time in keeping track of your receivables, and should be able to easily display the status of any customer account. Whether you have a manual or computerized system, your accounts receivable ledger is one of your most valuable business tools and should always be kept strictly up to date. It gives you a permanent listing of every one of your customer accounts and tells you the current status and amount of activity in each.

With a manual system, you simply copy the current balance onto one of the commercially available, preprinted statement forms at the end of the month. Choose a set of preprinted statement forms that has at least two parts to it. Send the original to the customer and keep a duplicate for your records (see Sample 6). With a computerized system, you can easily generate printed statements anytime, though month's end is the usual time to send them out to customers.

You should deposit all cash and checks as soon as possible after they are received. With a manual system, be sure to record customer payments in your deposit book so that the account can be correctly credited. Some accounting packages will automatically credit a customer's account when a payment is deposited. However you do it, make certain that customer payments are credited correctly and promptly. Mistakes here can be costly in terms of lost customer goodwill.

d. Expenses

Keep a detailed record of all your expenses as they occur. Don't rely on your memory to recall amounts that you have paid out. Always ask for receipts. At times this is a nuisance, but you must do it if you want the expenditure to count as a business expense. In those few cases where it is not possible to get a receipt (e.g., parking), jot down the expense in your notebook.

If you attend an out-of-town craft show, bring an envelope with you and stuff into it your receipts for meals, motel bills, gas, etc. When you get back home, you can sort out the different kinds of expenses and write yourself a business check for those items that you have paid for out of cash from your own pocket.

Whenever possible, pay your bills by check so that your canceled checks can serve as receipts. Retain all your supplier's invoices. File these away alphabetically in an accordion file or in file folders so that

SAMPLE STATEMENT

STATEMENT

Rockinghorse Crafts Ltd.

Tantallon R.R. 2, Site 4, Box 7, N.S. B0J 3J0

Tel. (902) 835-5287

TERMS
NET 30 DAYS
2% per month
interest on
overdue accounts

DATE _____

ABC Craft Shop
123 Main St.
Anytown, N.Y. 10019

DATE	DETAILS	DEBIT		CREDIT		BALANCE		
May 25	INV. # 1034	442	50			442	50	Dr.

you can retrieve them easily if you want to verify expenses, check supplier prices or terms, or gather any other information you might need.

e. Journals and the General Ledger

Your manual bookkeeping system will be simpler if you keep all your figures in one big journal. I know many books on accounting refer to sales journals, cash disbursement journals, and others, but it is simpler and easier for a small craft business, especially when starting out, to keep everything in one big journal. (Accountants call this the synoptic journal.) Be sure to buy a big one with at least 24 columns across.

Since more and more businesses have adopted computerized accounting systems, it may be difficult in some places to purchase the large multi-column journals, and you may be obliged to use several separate journals, but the principles remain the same. For the illustration in Sample 7, I have used a synoptic journal because it is easier for demonstration purposes to have everything in one place. Sample 7 shows how to head the columns and how to enter information in such a journal. As you can see, each amount is entered twice, once as a credit and once as a debit. No matter how many entries you make, the sum of the debit and credit entries should always be equal, providing you with an automatic check on the accuracy of your figures.

In our illustration, we do not enter cash (i.e., recognize it in our system) until it is deposited in the bank. Each of the major income and expense items has a column of its own. We have entered only a few; you can have as many as you like (e.g., truck, operating supplies).

To understand the meaning of debits and credits, think of each transaction as involving a side that "gives" and a side that "receives" something. A debit entry is made in the account that receives and a credit entry is made in the account that gives. The first transaction in Sample 7 is a cash sale, the results of a craft market. In it the bank receives (is debited with) $550, which is given by (is credited to) sales ($500) and sales tax ($50). The other transactions are described underneath the sample.

Don't despair if you don't grasp the nature of debits and credits the first time around. Before entering into business, I had steeped myself thoroughly in the liberal arts (philosophy and history) and

SAMPLE 7
SYNOPTIC JOURNAL

MAY 199-

DATE	DESCRIPTION	CK. #S	BANK DR.	BANK CR.	A/C RECEIVABLE DR.	A/C RECEIVABLE CR.	SALES CR.	SALES TAX CR.	FREIGHT DR.	FREIGHT CR.	PURCHASES DR.	OFFICE SUPPLIES DR.	A/C PAYABLE DR.	A/C PAYABLE CR.
MAY 2	1. Riverside Craft Market		550.00				500.00	50.00						
MAY 2	2. ABC Shop				250.00		240.00			10.00				
MAY 5	3. Zy Shop		175.00			175.00								
MAY 7	4. Fleecy Wool Co.										120.00			120.00
MAY 8	5. Jill's Stationery	89		45.00								45.00		

1. You make a cash sale. The bank is debited with $550; $500 is credited to sales and $50 is credited to sales tax.

2. You sell a customer goods on credit. Accounts receivable is debited with $250; sales is credited with $240 and freight (which you paid for but intend to charge to the customer) is credited with $10.

3. A customer pays you $175 for goods you shipped last month. You debit the bank with $175 and credit accounts receivable with $175.

4. You buy $120 worth of raw materials on credit. You debit purchases with $120 and credit accounts payable with $120.

5. You pay (by check) a $45 bill for stationery supplies you received on credit last month. You debit accounts payable with $45 and credit bank with $45.

totally ignored the crass world of commerce. I thought debits and credits were some kind of breakfast cereal, but it didn't take me long to find out otherwise.

Once you've made a few entries (especially when using real money for practice) you'll quickly get the hang of it, and soon you'll begin to wonder why they never taught it to you at school.

Each of the columns in your journal will have a separate account or page in your general ledger. Entries in the general ledger are usually made at the end of each month. If you are using accounting software, the computer does most of the work for you. Whether you use a manual or a computerized system, however, you should get your accountant to help you set up the general ledger in the beginning and to explain to you how financial statements are produced. This may involve several fairly lengthy sessions with your accountant, but it is worthwhile. By having a complete understanding of your financial records, you will be able to make your business run more efficiently and make bigger profits.

Whether you do your accounting manually or use accounting software, the underlying principles are exactly the same. With a computerized system, the actual work of doing your accounting is, of course, much easier because the program does most of the repetitious work, such as balancing and carrying totals and subtotals from one place to another. Good accounting software means much less chance of error, and once data are entered into the system, you have all the critical information for running your business right at your fingertips whenever you need it.

Setting up a computerized accounting system or converting a manual one does take some time. If you plan to do either, you should pick a quiet time of the year — this is definitely not a project you should undertake during the pre-Christmas or Spring rush season.

f. Depreciation

If you buy an important piece of equipment or make an addition to your workshop, you make a special kind of entry in your records. Real property and equipment constitute fixed assets. These are not used or consumed in the same way as your materials, but a part of their useful life goes into the production of each one of your products. It would not be realistic to consider the whole cost of a fixed asset as an expense in any one year. Instead, the cost of the asset is distributed over the period of its useful life. This is known as depreciation of the asset. Your electric kiln, wood lathe, or loom as well as your workshop, vehicle, and other fixed assets will last only a certain number of years. At the end of that time, you will have to replace them.

Depreciation is an important factor in calculating your year-end profit and income tax. For income tax purposes, various kinds of fixed assets are grouped together in classes and yearly depreciation is allowed at a certain rate prescribed by the tax department. Certain types of production equipment can, for example, be written off in a year or two.

Yearly depreciation rates for the most common types of fixed assets are available from the tax department (the IRS or Revenue Canada) or you can get them from your accountant. The amount that you choose to write off in your yearly financial statement may be different from the amount used for income tax purposes. This is a highly complex subject beyond the scope of this book; seek the advice of your accountant.

g. Payroll

If you are employing others or if your business is incorporated, you are responsible for deductions at source from your employees' wages or salaries. You must open an account with the tax department and they will send you a book of tables of the amounts that you must deduct for each pay period. To keep track of this with a manual system, use a separate payroll book with columns for the various types of deductions. If you opt for a computerized system, make certain that the payroll module in the package you choose has the capacity to handle all the entries and deductions you are required to make, both federally and in your own state or province.

h. Taxes

We have already looked at the reasons for keeping accurate and up-to-date records and some of the mechanics of record keeping. As mentioned earlier, one of the main reasons for having a good bookkeeping system is to avoid paying any more taxes than you absolutely have to.

Since the tax laws are not only extremely complex but are constantly being changed, it is absolutely necessary for the small-business

NOT DECLARING INCOME EARNED FROM YOUR BUSINESS IS TAX FRAUD, PURE AND SIMPLE.

person to seek tax advice from an accountant. However, just as in the area of record keeping, there are quite a number of things that you can do yourself to reduce the tax bite.

1. Income

In the area of what to include as income there is not much scope for tax saving. Not declaring income earned from your business is tax fraud, pure and simple. Apart from being illegal, not declaring income can be highly disadvantageous if you are applying for a loan. There may come a time when the continued success or even survival of your business will depend on getting a loan. No respectable lender will give you money on the basis of your word that your financial records have to be seen in the light of the extra income you do not declare on your tax return!

A similar situation would arise if you wanted to sell your business; you couldn't seriously expect a potential buyer to offer a big price for your business on the basis that you cheat on your income tax.

2. Expenses

In the area of expenses, there is more scope for tax saving. Keep receipts for all business expenses and personal expenses where any portion of the expense can be charged to your business. Though simple and obvious, this rule is often ignored, either because people find it too much trouble to ask for receipts or because they believe that certain expenses will be allowed without them.

If it is not too much trouble earning your income in the first place, it certainly isn't too much trouble to ask for a receipt. It's this simple: every time you keep the receipt for $2 spent on postage or parking or whatever, you put another tax-free dollar into your pocket.

There are very few places where you simply cannot get a receipt for expenditures. Where this does happen, as in the case of pay-telephone calls or parking meters, you should keep a diary of these expenses. I said this earlier, but it bears repeating. You would be surprised how some of these minor expenses can add up to quite significant amounts in a year's time.

If you believe that you are entitled to claim certain expenses without substantiating receipts, you are completely wrong. Your mistake could turn out to be a costly one. Without receipts, a tax assessor does not have to allow a single cent for your expenses, no matter what they are. In the case of relatively small amounts paid for by cash, you must be particularly careful. While on a sales trip or attending an out-of-town craft market, always ask for and keep all your receipts for meals and lodging. Keep a detailed diary of expenses for parking, postage, pay telephones, and similar small amounts.

(a) Automobile expenses

Both the IRS and Revenue Canada require that all vehicle expenses be recorded and kept. It is not sufficient just to write down expenses incurred when you were actually using the vehicle for business. You must keep the entire year's expenses, including fuel, repairs, insurance, parking, depreciation, interest on the vehicle loan, license, and registration fees. If you use your vehicle for both business and pleasure, you then allocate the total vehicle expenses to your business on the basis of business miles traveled to total miles traveled.

(b) Business expenses in the home

One of the many advantages of operating your craft business from your home is the ability to deduct a certain portion of your home expenses, such as heat, rent, taxes, utilities, and mortgage. In Canada, mortgage interest payments are not normally deductible for private residences, so anything you can do to make a portion deductible will result in significant tax benefits.

In order to deduct a portion of your home expenses, you are required to establish that you regularly use a specific part of the home for your craft business. Once this is established, you can deduct the portion of items, such as rent and heat, assignable to that portion of the home. But be careful here. In order to qualify for a tax deduction, a room must be used solely for business purposes. You cannot, for example, claim office expenses for an "office" that occupies a part of your bedroom.

(c) Maintenance and repairs

Maintenance refers to the routine painting of a building or replacement of parts on machinery and equipment. Repairs means fixing a breakdown or restoring something to normal mechanical condition. The value of a repair can be claimed as a business expense in the year it was incurred.

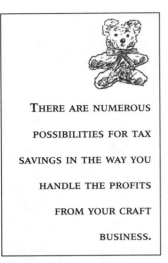

What happens in the case of very extensive repairs? If you have a flat roof that leaks, you may decide that rather than have it patched up, you will have a pitched roof built over the building. In this case, there will be an addition to the building, even though it was prompted by the need for a repair.

The difference from the tax point of view is that a repair can be claimed as an expense in the current year, while an addition has to be added to the capital cost of the asset and depreciated over a number of years. Also, if the addition is depreciated and the asset is subsequently sold for more than the depreciated value, there is a "recapture" of depreciation and tax has to be paid on the recapture.

Naturally, it is to your advantage as a taxpayer to "expense" an item whenever possible. If in doubt about whether an item can be treated this way, check with your accountant.

3. Profits

There are numerous possibilities for tax savings in the way you handle the profits from your craft business. If you are operating your business under your own name, all the profits of the business are considered to be your income and they are taxed in your name. It is possible to split the income from your business among family members by putting your spouse and children on the payroll. Chapter 14 discusses the various forms of business organization and suggests ways of saving taxes by splitting income among family members.

Say you want to take out $28,000 in salary from your business in a given year. The tax bite is obviously much less if you and your spouse each take $14,000, but in order to take full advantage of these tax-saving possibilities, certain conditions must be met (see chapter 14).

If your business is incorporated, there are further possibilities of tax saving. Because you and your company are separate and distinct legal entities, it is possible to leave a portion of your profits in the company to use for whatever company purpose you choose. However, this only saves taxes when the corporate rate of taxation is less than your personal rate. This is frequently the case in Canada where small, Canadian-owned private corporations that meet certain conditions are entitled to special tax rates of 15 percent to 27 percent. (Also, in Canada there is a further 5 percent reduction in the corporate tax rate for manufacturers, which includes almost all craft businesses.)

Instead of withdrawing money from your company in the form of salaries for yourself or other members of your family, it is possible to take money out of the company in the form of dividends. There is also a disadvantage to this, however. Since dividends are subject to taxes in both the United States and Canada, the net effect is that these withdrawals are subject to double taxation: once when the company earns the money, and again when the money is paid out. In certain circumstances, it is still advantageous from a tax point of view to withdraw money from your company in the form of dividends, but check first with your accountant.

i. You and Your Accountant

When it comes to income tax advice, don't rely on bookkeepers. Their expertise is limited to the organization of information into the standard accounting forms. For tax matters you should seek the services of a professional accountant who can advise you how to minimize tax payable and maximize profit in light of the most recent rules and regulations. These rules and regulations are not only highly complex, they are constantly changing.

What you can do to minimize the accounting fee is to have all your routine bookkeeping done so that you don't pay a high-priced accountant to do mundane tasks you could easily do yourself or have a spouse or employee do. You can also be aware of the various possible areas for tax saving as outlined above so that you can ask specific questions of your accountant about what is best in your particular circumstances.

Choosing an accountant is as important as choosing your doctor or lawyer. You want someone with a good professional reputation who also makes you feel comfortable. Avoid anyone who can converse only in unintelligible accountant's jargon or who bills you for a telephone conference if you call to clarify a minor point on the telephone. Look for a professional who regularly deals with and understands the needs of small businesses and is prepared to help you set up a simple manual or computerized system along the lines recommended in this chapter.

If you don't know where to start looking, ask your bank manager or a business acquaintance if they can recommend someone. Don't be afraid to talk to several accountants before making a choice and don't hesitate to ask about their fees. A good accountant can actually save you far more than his or her fee, but that doesn't mean you don't need to know the size of the fee in advance.

Chapter 14

MANAGING YOUR CRAFT BUSINESS

a. Business Organization

The form of organization of your craft business is not likely to occupy a lot of your time in the beginning, nor should it. There are more important things to do, like getting your business off and running. Before too long, however, you should give some thought to the structure of your business.

The main reason for this is that it allows you to plan for the future. This planning will provide for the easy development of your business. As your income rises, you may want to begin expanding your business, perhaps employing assistants or enlarging your workshop. These moves can lead to increased capital or production costs, which can be very hard to handle for a business that is not organized.

There are three possible forms of organization for a small craft business. Your business may be run as a sole proprietorship, a partnership, or an incorporated company.

1. The sole proprietorship

Most small craft businesses operate as sole proprietorships. This is the simplest form of business organization. No legal papers are required, there are no extra expenses, you have only yourself to blame if things

go wrong, and you take all the profits if you succeed. The tax consequences are also the simplest. Whatever the business makes is counted as your personal income, and you pay taxes on it accordingly.

A sole proprietorship can be operated legally under your own name without registration, but if you want to adopt a distinctive name for your business, as many craftspeople do, it is advisable to register it. This is a very simple procedure. For the specific requirements in your locality, contact the county clerk's office or state/provincial companies office.

2.   The partnership

A partnership is a slightly more complex form of business organization than the sole proprietorship. Legal expenses are minimal, but a partnership should include a written agreement with your partner, which should then be registered as a proper legal document.

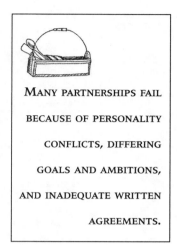

MANY PARTNERSHIPS FAIL BECAUSE OF PERSONALITY CONFLICTS, DIFFERING GOALS AND AMBITIONS, AND INADEQUATE WRITTEN AGREEMENTS.

Sometimes partnerships work out extremely well, especially when each partner brings specific expertise or skills to the business that the other partner lacks. A good combination could be that of a skilled designer/craftsperson together with someone who has a flair for marketing. On the other hand, many partnerships fail because of personality conflicts, differing goals and ambitions, and inadequate written agreements.

A fertile area for disagreements between craft business partners is the size of the business. As a craft business grows, one of the partners may feel that the commercial side of the operation tends to overshadow the creative, artistic side. This is a frequent conflict when partners have different goals for the business.

A major drawback to the partnership form of organization is that each partner assumes unlimited liability for all debts incurred in the business. This means unlimited personal liability. In other words, should the business fail, creditors can claim against the personal assets of one or all of the partners.

3.   The corporation

A corporation is a separate, legal entity. Setting it up involves some paperwork and incorporation fees and may require legal help. The rules of incorporation vary in different states and provinces in the degree of complexity, the number of persons required to form a corporation, and the costs. Some states and provinces permit an individual to incorporate.

"Incorporation kits" are available which permit you to do much of the legal work yourself and greatly reduce the cost of incorporating.

One of the biggest advantages of the corporate form is the limited liability of the shareholder for debts of the company. Each shareholder's liability is limited to the amount of money individually invested. Creditors of the company have no claims against the personal assets of shareholders.

In actual practice, however, not all of the advantages of limited liability are available to the small corporation. Where loans to the company are involved, banks and other financial institutions may require that owners or shareholders provide personal guarantees. This, in effect, nullifies the advantages of limited liability as far as your obligations to the bank are concerned.

There are some tax advantages to the corporate form of business organization. You do not need to incorporate to be able to deduct a salary paid to your spouse, but by incorporation it is possible to pay wages or salaries to other members of your family as well. However, you must be able to show that they performed specific duties and that the remuneration paid was reasonable.

A craftsperson can withdraw money either as salary/wages or in the form of dividends. As income rises and the person's marginal rate of taxation increases, it is sometimes advantageous to withdraw money from the company in the form of dividends where the effective rate of taxation is less than it would be if the money were taxed as salary. This is a highly complex area and before making a decision about incorporating, it is best to seek the advice of a tax accountant.

Self-Counsel Press publishes incorporation guides and forms for Washington, British Columbia, Alberta, and Ontario.

b. Financial Planning

You must be certain that you have enough cash on hand for your day-to-day operations. You may have a good product and sales that have grown to the point where you have hired an assistant, but still find yourself chronically short of ready cash to pay your bills or to withdraw sufficient money for your personal needs.

Cash management is relatively simple if all your sales are on a cash basis. If you sell $5,000 worth of products in May, you know you will receive $5,000 the same month. If, however, a large part of your business is done on credit, you would not receive the $5,000 until some later time. How much later would depend on your credit terms and the extent to which your customers adhere to them. If you have a large financial commitment to meet in May, say a down payment on a new piece of equipment, you will need to know just how much cash you can expect to come in during May. You need to prepare a cash flow statement.

A cash flow statement is simply a way of setting out clearly the timing and amounts of cash income and cash payments. A typical cash flow statement for a craft business might look like the one in Sample 8. This is for the period from May to the end of the year. (Any time period can be chosen.) We have also shown projected financial transactions (i.e., how much the business will have to borrow and when it will be able to repay its operating loans). This is the kind of information you would need to provide to a lender when applying for a loan.

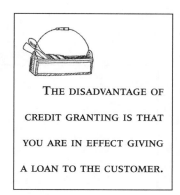

THE DISADVANTAGE OF CREDIT GRANTING IS THAT YOU ARE IN EFFECT GIVING A LOAN TO THE CUSTOMER.

c. Giving Credit to Your Customers

At some point, you will have to face the question of whether to grant credit to your customers. Most production craft businesses do grant credit, and you may have to follow suit if you want to remain competitive. The main advantage of granting credit is that it increases sales by allowing goods to be purchased by retailers who would otherwise be unable to do so. This, in turn, helps the retailers to buy a little extra and thereby increase their own sales.

The disadvantage of credit granting is that you are in effect giving a loan to the customer. You incur all the costs of production but you do not receive payment until some time later. This means you must have more capital available than if you did business strictly on a cash basis. In addition, there are the costs of keeping records, billing, and collecting your money. There is also the possibility that some customers won't pay and you will end up with a bad debt expense.

If you decide to grant credit to your customers, you should try to minimize the disadvantages by doing the following:

(i)   Make sure that the costs of granting credit are built into your prices. This will be difficult to do exactly, but you should estimate the various extra costs, particularly paperwork, involved in credit sales and factor these into your prices.

(ii) The risks of granting credit can be greatly reduced by establishing a set of rules and sticking strictly to them. Decide what terms you will offer and who will qualify for credit.

SAMPLE 8
CASH FLOW STATEMENT

BEST MADE WOOD CRAFT CO. INC.

CASH FLOW PROJECTIONS AND PROJECTED FINANCIAL TRANSACTIONS

	1	2	3	4	5	6	7	8
	MAY	JUNE	JULY	AUGUST	SEPT.	OCT.	NOV.	DEC.
1 Sales	18,000	20,000	22,000	18,000	18,000	29,000	29,000	20,000
2 Collections on account	14,500	16,000	19,000	21,000	20,000	27,000	28,000	20,000
3 Other cash receipts	3,400	1,400	1,400	1,400	440	440	440	440
4 Total cash receipts	17,900	17,400	20,400	22,400	20,440	27,440	28,440	20,440
5 Purchases	10,000	4,000	4,000	4,000	4,000	4,000	4,000	4,000
6 Wages & Salaries	6,000	6,800	6,800	6,800	6,800	6,800	6,800	6,800
7 Accounting	100	100	100	100	100	100	100	100
8 Advertising & Shows	1,500	1,100						
9 Electricity	125	140	140	140	140	140	140	140
10 Fuel	100	75	50	50	50	75	100	100
11 Insurance (paid in 2 installments)	1,250	1,250						
12 Interest (long term)	708	708	708	708	708	708	708	708
13 Operating supplies	300	300	300	300	300	400	400	300
14 Repairs & maintenance	200	200	200	200	200	200	200	200
15 Taxes	200	200	200	200	200	200	200	200
16 Telephone	90	90	90	90	90	90	90	90
17 Truck	200	200	200	200	200	200	200	200
18 Sales taxes	1,260	1,620	1,800	1,980	1,620	1,620	2,610	2,610
19 Pre-paid freight	720	800	880	720	720	1,160	1,160	800
20 Sales staff commissions	450	2,100	2,490	2,460	2,160	2,250	2,400	2,400
21 Bank loan interest	140	210	247	227	178	136	25	—
22 Total monthly expenses	23,343	19,893	18,205	18,175	17,466	18,079	19,133	18,648
23 Net monthly cash surplus [deficit]	[5443]	[2,493]	2,195	4,225	2,974	9,361	9,307	1,792
24 Borrowing to maintain $1,000 min. bal.	6,000	3,000	—	0	—	—	—	—
25 Cumulative borrowing ($11,000 at end of April)	17,000	20,000	18,000	14,000	11,000	2,000	—	—

Net 30 days is the most common payment period in the craft/gift-ware business. You may want to offer a discount for cash payment or for payment within 10 days. You must also decide what action you will take if accounts become overdue and what interest rate you will charge. Both rates for discounts and interest charge penalties should be slightly higher than the current rate you are paying to your bank for commercial loans.

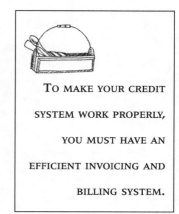

TO MAKE YOUR CREDIT SYSTEM WORK PROPERLY, YOU MUST HAVE AN EFFICIENT INVOICING AND BILLING SYSTEM.

The best way to establish the credit-worthiness of new customers is to ask them to fill out a credit questionnaire. This need be no more than a typewritten sheet that you can photocopy. It should include space for their name, address, and telephone number, length of time at that address, bank name and address, and credit references.

Ask for the names of at least three suppliers with whom the customer is currently doing business, and make sure you take the time to check these out. You must find out the length of time the supplier has been doing business with the customer, the size of the customer's credit limit, the supplier's credit terms, and the past pattern of payments by the customer. This can be done by mail or over the telephone. If your customer is in a big hurry, you should request payment in advance for the first order or permission to ship the order C.O.D.

To make your credit system work properly, you must have an efficient invoicing and billing system (see chapter 13). If you neglect to send out bills, some of your customers are almot certain to neglect to send in their payments. Your accounts receivable should be monitored regularly to detect those that have become overdue. A prompt reminder to a delinquent account will usually get you a payment. When this does not happen, you should get on the telephone and find out why.

During your collection call, be tactful and polite but firm. Perhaps your customer has simply forgotten to pay. In most instances your call will prompt the customer to pay. Where this does not bring the desired result, you ought to consider handing the account over to a collection agency, but do this only as a last resort if all other efforts to collect the account fail. The best way to protect yourself against the risk of non-payment is to have a sound credit policy to begin with and to carry out detailed credit checks on your customers.

d. Insurance

Insurance is something you cannot afford to be without. If you and your family are dependent upon the earnings from your craft business, you should provide yourself with as much protection as possible.

You are certainly going to need fire and theft coverage on your building, tools, and inventory. As your inventory is likely to fluctuate from month to month, it is a good idea to investigate a stock coverage policy that allows for these fluctuations. With this kind of coverage, your premiums for insurance on your stock reflect the amount of inventory actually on hand at the end of each month.

Third-party insurance is also necessary, particularly if you have a retail operation. This will protect you if a lawsuit arises out of an injury that someone sustains on your premises for which you might be held responsible. You should also consider insurance to protect you against suits that could arise from product defects and insurance against loss of income that may result from an interruption in your business due to some unforeseen disaster. Disability insurance will cover you for any permanent injury.

Life insurance has been described as a way of keeping you poor all your life so that you can die rich. Nonetheless, you should seriously consider at least some life insurance if you have a family; more can be added as your income grows. Endowment insurance will pay the whole amount of the policy directly to you if you survive beyond a specified date or to your beneficiary if you die before that time. This kind of insurance can also serve as collateral for a loan.

Insurance is expensive. You should shop around for it as you would for any other "big ticket" item in your budget. Use an insurance agent who deals with many different insurance companies and who will spend some time with you going over your needs and checking with the various companies on prices.

If you are operating a craft business at home, tell your insurance agent. Don't assume that your home or tenant policy will cover your business assets for loss by fire or theft. Not informing your insurance company that you are carrying on a business in your house could also invalidate your home policy.

e. Your Craft Business and Your Family

Going into business for yourself involves not just a job but a particular lifestyle. You have much greater freedom of choice than the person who is employed by someone else. You control your hours of work and working conditions, and you must regularly make decisions about matters most people take for granted. You are more likely to succeed in your own business if you are the type of person who enjoys decision making. You also need to be able to live sensibly with your greater freedom, neither wasting your time nor wearing yourself out with too much work.

We have already mentioned the many advantages of working at home; however, working at home calls for more self-discipline than if you went out to work. You are responsible to yourself. You can work at any time of the day or night, but your craft business must also co-exist with the other members of your family. If your family is not directly involved in your business and you work at home, you will have to make it clear that when you are at work, you are not available for family chores. You should set aside certain hours of the day when you are at work in your studio or workshop; during that time it should be understood that you are not to be disturbed.

It may be possible to involve your family in your business. One of the unique features of a craft business is the way in which it can lend itself to family participation. Sometimes both partners are involved directly in craft design and production. Or, if only one partner is actually producing, the spouse can be of assistance selling at craft markets, running your retail outlet, or doing the books.

Your family can help out at craft markets and at a variety of jobs around the workshop. Even quite young children can be of assistance, helping at craft markets, cleaning the workshop, stuffing envelopes, filling boxes.

If you are employing your spouse and/or children regularly, part of the income from your craft business can be split among family members, thereby lessening your tax burden. Be careful, however, to pay family members in proportion to what they actually do. Amounts paid to your spouse and children must be reasonable or they will not be allowed by the tax department. As a general rule, you should pay members of your family the same amounts you would have to pay hired help to do the same jobs. Also make certain that you pay them at regular intervals and that they have their own bank accounts.

Involving members of your family in your craft business is only worthwhile if your family enjoys it. Some craftspeople can't bear to have their spouse or children around them while they work; some spouses and children don't necessarily want to work in a family business. The extent to which your spouse and/or children should get involved in your craft business obviously depends very much on how well everyone gets along.

Chapter 15

EXPANDING YOUR CRAFT BUSINESS

a. How Big Do You Want to Be?

We have already mentioned the tremendous variety possible in the craft world. In effect, you can be as small or as big as you wish. Just how big can you be? Well, if the conditions are right, that is, you have a really good product and the entrepreneurial ability to develop and market it, you can build your craft business into a substantial company with hundreds of employees and sales in the millions.

There are literally thousands of firms today that are essentially craft businesses, though we tend generally not to think of them as such. Most of the famous British and European potteries, for example, are large-scale craft industries. In North America, there are thousands of handcraft companies making everything from alligator purses to ornamental zarfs. (Incidentally, a zarf is a metal cup-shaped holder used to hold a hot coffee cup.) Some of these are well known, others less so. Many of them would rank as substantial enterprises anywhere in terms of sales and employment figures.

However, the vast majority of craft businesses are small, consisting of just the owner and sometimes one or two employees. The owners of most small craft businesses prefer to keep them that way.

Building a large enterprise means taking a lot of risks. It also involves a completely different lifestyle. In the small craft enterprise, even where there are employees, the owner/manager generally works in the studio along with everyone else. In a larger operation, the owner/manager would most probably not be involved directly in the production side of the operation.

Whether a particular craft business can operate on a greatly increased scale depends on a variety of factors. One of the most important is the product itself. Unless the product has some inherent features that distinguish it as a handmade piece, it will not be able to compete in the marketplace with either domestic factory-made goods or cheap (largely handmade) imported goods. There is no one single identifying feature that gives a product this characteristic, handcrafted appeal. It may lie in the exceptionally high quality of the work, the obvious attention to detail, the intricacy or beauty of the design, or even the buyer's knowledge that the piece was made by hand rather than turned out by a machine.

If you think it is possible for you to sell vastly greater quantities of your product and you personally are prepared to go into large-scale production, there are some things you should investigate first. We shall look at each of these below.

A HIGHER VOLUME OF SALES DOES NOT NECESSARILY MEAN HIGHER PROFITS.

1. Rate of growth

Look at the rate of growth of your business to date. In a small craft business, it is not uncommon to have growth rates of 200 percent or 300 percent or even higher in the first few years. Be careful to view this in the proper perspective. You started out very small, perhaps part time. It is much easier to achieve a given percentage increase on a smaller base. If first-year sales from your part-time business were $10,000, you would only need to sell another $10,000 worth of products to double your sales. If you are selling $50,000 worth, you obviously need a much larger absolute increase in business in order to double your sales. A fairly obvious point, but you'd be surprised how often it tends to be overlooked.

2. Profitability

A higher volume of sales does not necessarily mean higher profits. This is again a fairly obvious point, though it is sometimes learned the hard way. I know of a craft operation with sales in the area of a quarter of a million dollars. The owner recently confessed to me that the after-tax profit is actually less than what it was when he worked on his own and sold $50,000 worth of products in a year.

3. Lifestyle

A business with employees is substantially different from one where you work entirely on your own or with members of your family. Besides the additional complications of dealing with employees and the extra paperwork, there is a certain loss of privacy when you have hired workers on the premises. As well, some craftspeople feel that by enlarging their businesses, the commercial side overshadows the creative side of their operations.

4. The market

Will expansion mean selling more products in the same market or will you have to open up new markets farther afield? Remember the point made earlier about not approaching saturation in any given market area. As the volume sold in a given market area increases, it will eventually reach a point where the product begins to lose its appeal because there is simply too much in that market. There are very few handcrafted products to which this would not apply, although the saturation point is naturally different for different products. If your planned expansion means opening new markets, you must consider how best to do this. Will you expand both wholesale and retail sides of your business? Will you use your existing marketing channels, or do you have to consider new ones? How will you ship your products into the new market?

5. Quality

If expansion means that you make much larger quantities of product, you must ensure that the quality remains high. Since you cannot produce the larger quantities yourself, maintaining quality depends on motivating your employees to produce according to your own exacting standards. This can be a tricky task, but you have to find ways of doing it. (See *Motivating Today's Employees,* also published by Self-Counsel Press.) You must also have methods of monitoring quality to make sure that standards are consistently maintained.

b. Forecasting

1. Why forecast?

If you are planning to expand your craft business, you should prepare an operating forecast to see what will happen to your income and your costs. Generally, a forecast is done for a one-year period, though you could choose a longer or a shorter period if you wish.

A FORECAST NEED NOT BE

A TERRIBLY COMPLEX

AFFAIR.

A forecast can be of benefit to you in several ways. It can help you distinguish between the various alternatives open to you — to put up a new workshop or renovate and enlarge the old building, to hire additional employees, and other decisions that will affect the future of your business. For example, you might discover a steadily increasing trend of retail sales from your own studio. You may not have paid too much attention to these because they were a relatively small percentage of your total sales. You might now want to consider setting up a separate retail outlet apart from your studio and possibly carry the work of other craftspeople as well as your own.

A forecast also forces you to look ahead and consider the overall financial position of your business. You may become aware of opportunities and concerns that are not apparent in the day-to-day operation of the business.

Suppose you find that, despite an increase in sales, profits have been declining. You will then want to look very carefully at your expenses to see which of these has been showing a tendency to increase.

2. Preparing a forecast

A forecast need not be a terribly complex affair. What you do is simply set out what you reasonably expect to happen to your revenue and expenses if certain changes take place.

Think carefully about what your business can reasonably be expected to do. Be totally realistic. Naturally, you hope for big increases in sales, but when doing your forecast, you have to be guided by reasonable expectations based on past results. Start with your last year's operating statement. Then determine all the changes you plan to make and the effects these changes will have on your revenues, expenses, and profits.

Suppose you are planning to purchase a more expensive loom and hire an employee to work with you. These changes will mean a substantial increase in output, but the increase won't materialize right away. However, your expenses will increase immediately.

You are currently selling all the work you can produce, and yearly sales are about $50,000. You anticipate sales of about $100,000 on the basis of the following points:

(i) Your sales doubled last year over the previous year and your business is still in the early stages of growth.

(ii) You are getting a lot of repeat orders.

(iii) You expect more orders from a major trade show at which you plan to exhibit.

(iv) You have just hired a sales representative.

(v) The general economic picture is beginning to look better than it has for some time.

Samples 9 and 10 show how your operating statement for the current year and your forecast for the following year might look.

If you are convinced that expansion will mean increased profitability and you are prepared for the lifestyle changes that expansion usually brings, you have to consider the means by which you can carry out your expansion plans. If you plan to invest in a larger building and/or new tools and equipment, you have to arrange financing. You will have to hire and train people to work for you. You will have to open up new markets for your products. Be sure to read the chapters in this book that cover those areas.

OPERATING STATEMENT

For the Year Ending December 31, 200-

SALES	$50,000	
Raw materials	12,500	
Wages (paid to yourself)	12,500	
Gross profit		25,000
EXPENSES		
Accounting	500	
Advertising and shows	700	
Depreciation	800	
Electricity and fuel	1,200	
Freight	600	
Insurance	1,400	
Interest	3,200	
Miscellaneous	500	
Operating supplies	500	
Repairs	250	
Telephone	600	
Truck	2,000	
		12,250
Net profit		12,750

SAMPLE 10
OPERATING FORECAST

For the Year Ending December 31, 200-

SALES	$100,000	
Raw materials	25,000	
Wages (paid to yourself)	25,000	
Gross profit		50,000
EXPENSES		
Accounting	500	
Advertising and shows	2,100	
Depreciation	2,000	
Electricity and fuel	1,800	
Freight	1,200	
Insurance	2,200	
Interest	4,000	
Miscellaneous	1,000	
Operating supplies	600	
Repairs	300	
Sales commissions	10,500	
Telephone	800	
Truck	2,400	
		29,400
Net profit		20,600

Chapter 16

EMPLOYEES: HOW TO HIRE AND TRAIN THEM

a. Do You Need to Hire Anyone?

As a general rule, you should not employ anyone in your craft business until you absolutely have to. The only exception to this is when you hire your spouse or children to help out. Before hiring anyone else, you should first look at the situation very carefully to be sure that it is really necessary. Perhaps you can reorganize your work, hire your spouse to do the bookkeeping, or speed up aspects of the work process.

Becoming an employer can radically change the nature of your business in a number of ways. When you hire employees, you become involved in many complex rules and regulations. There are laws governing hours of labor, minimum wages, and working conditions. You are obliged to collect payroll taxes. There are more government forms to fill out. Unless you are very fortunate in finding someone already qualified, you will have to invest time and money in training. Moreover, you may go to all the trouble of training someone only to have that person quit just after he or she has finished the training. Or your ex-employee may promptly go and set up a business in competition with yours.

However, most of these problems can be minimized if you go about the business of hiring in a systematic and clear-headed way.

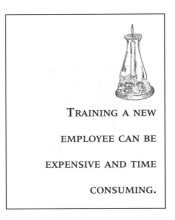

There is an absolute upper limit on what you can produce yourself. If you use hired help, you can greatly increase your output. You can delegate some of the more routine jobs to others and concentrate your own efforts on those tasks that call for the highest levels of skill. By freeing yourself from production in this way, you can also spend more time on design and marketing. You can frequently produce a higher-quality product by producing in quantity.

b. Hiring Employees

If it is possible to hire trained workers, you won't have to worry about training. In most cases, however, you will have to spend time training new employees. Most craft businesses produce a product which, even if it is not really unique, is so highly specialized that it is difficult to find workers who can produce it without at least some training.

Naturally you would look for people with some previous training or experience in your own craft field. If you are a potter, you'd look for someone with at least a modicum of experience in pottery. If you are a metalworker, you'd look for someone with metalwork knowledge, and so on.

Training someone is expensive. You will be obliged to pay a novice the minimum wage or a wage that is comparable to the prevailing wage rates in your area. In the beginning, the new person will probably not produce enough salable work to pay his or her wages. In some cases, it is possible to get federal and state or provincial aid to train new employees, but the paperwork requirements for most government training programs are frequently so complicated that it is not worthwhile.

Training is also time consuming. Your output will initially be less than usual because of the time you have to spend training. This can be offset to some extent by having the trainee perform the more routine production tasks like loading the kiln, or nonproduction tasks like packing orders or taking inventory.

Many problems can be avoided if care is taken in the initial selection and hiring process. Don't rush out and hire the first person who is willing to work for you. A bad employee can make your life miserable and jeopardize the success of your business. Always look at more than one candidate for the job. Have a system of screening applicants. Don't just ask a job applicant to come talk to you about work until you have prepared yourself.

Be sure that you know exactly what you want the employee to do and what kind of employee you want. Always ask prospective employees to fill out an application, giving their educational qualifications and past job experience. Get the names and addresses of previous employers and call or write them for references. If you are likely to be hiring a number of employees, it is worthwhile drawing up a reference form. You can photocopy this and send it to former employers.

Ask previous employers to confirm the information given to you by the job applicant and ask about —

- the nature of the employee's duties while in their service,

- the reason why the employee left their service,

- whether they would rehire the person,

- their assessment of the person's ability to handle the job he or she is applying for,

- the applicant's ability to get along with others, and

- his or her willingness to accept supervision.

You might also ask them to rate the applicant (excellent, average, poor) in a number of specific categories: job performance, personality, neatness, attendance, and loyalty.

From the written applications, you should select the most promising candidates for interviews. Many craftspeople find job interviewing extremely difficult. Part of the reason is that they launch into it without sufficient preparation.

Jot down questions that you want to ask the candidate at the interview. During the interview, be as relaxed as possible and try to establish a comfortable, pleasant atmosphere. Be prepared to answer the candidate's questions about the nature of the job, but make sure that you retain control over the interview. Avoid a stand-offish, patronizing attitude but, at the same time, make it clear that the applicant is the person being evaluated.

After the initial interview, select the most promising two or three candidates and invite them to a second interview. Devise a simple, practical test for them involving some kind of work in your workshop. Obviously, this test depends on their skill level and experience. If they have previous experience, let them have a go at the wheel, lathe, or sewing machine. If they are beginners, give them something

IF YOU HIRE CARELESSLY, YOU ARE ONLY ASKING FOR TROUBLE.

very simple. Your objective is to find out their aptitude for the work and to determine how conscientious they are.

There are no surefire, 100 percent successful methods for selecting a good employee. When you have assembled all the relevant facts, you have to apply your own individual judgment. Is the person likely to be a good worker? Is he or she the kind of person you want to have around you? After all, it's your business and you want to work in a pleasant and relaxed atmosphere. You don't want hassles and tension in the workplace.

A new employee should be hired for a trial period of about six months. This is usually long enough for you to decide if you want to keep an employee. If there are going to be problems with the employee's work habits or attitude toward the job, these should become apparent before the end of the trial period.

Don't think that all of this is too much trouble. If you are serious about expanding your business, your success will depend to a large extent on your ability to recruit, train, and keep good, reliable, and honest employees. If you hire carelessly, you are only asking for trouble. A bungling, disgruntled, or dishonest employee can poison the work atmosphere, eat into the profits of your business, and destroy your peace of mind.

For more on hiring, see *The HR Book*, another title in the Self-Counsel Business Series.

c. Paying Your Employees

There are several different ways of going about paying employees in a craft business. You can pay your employees a fixed salary, an hourly wage, a piece rate, or some combination of these.

1. Salaries

If you have just one or two employees, you can pay them a fixed salary for a work week of a certain agreed-upon number of hours. (The hourly equivalent must, of course, be at least equal to the legal minimum wage for your state or province.) Obviously, you must be sure that the employee's weekly output is sufficient and that it is consistent.

2. Wages

The most common payment method is an hourly wage, paid weekly. How much you will have to offer more experienced workers will depend on the prevailing wage rates in your community. If you are to keep costs under control, you must figure out just how much work per hour you produce and set a reasonable standard for a new employee.

One of the most difficult aspects of the transition from a one-person craft business to a business with employees is in the area of cost control. There is no problem in controlling labor costs if you are doing all the work yourself. If you have employees, you must watch your labor costs continually.

3. Piece rate

Paying your employees so much per piece is an excellent way of keeping the lid on costs. It does require a bit more paperwork and, in the beginning at least, a lot of calculations in order to determine just how much to pay for each and every article that you are making. You must work with an hourly equivalent in mind and do your calculations so that a reasonably efficient, trained employee will make about the same that you would have to pay on an hourly basis.

The difference between an hourly-rate and a piece-rate system is that, having once worked out a set of piece rates, you will have automatic control of your labor costs. You also have a built-in incentive scheme, which will provide higher rewards to those workers who put forth a greater effort. You will, however, have to monitor the quality of work very carefully, but if the rates you set are realistic in terms of what your employees are capable of producing, quality need not suffer under a piece-rate system.

Even if you are paying your employees on a piece-rate basis, you will still have to pay hourly rates to people who are in training. Most new employees would not earn enough on a piece-rate basis to meet minimum wage requirements. It is possible to have hourly rates of pay for trainees and a piece-rate system for fully trained workers. However, you have to structure the piece rates so that there is an attractive differential between them and the hourly rates you pay a trainee. With a piece-rate system, a good employee can earn more than he or she would under an hourly system.

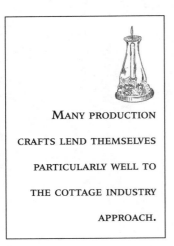

d. Profit Sharing

Profit sharing has been used as an incentive to productivity in all kinds and sizes of business. It can work with piece rates or an hourly wage system. By setting aside a certain proportion of profits (say 20 percent) for distribution among your employees, you can give them a sense of participation in the business and the feeling of working together as a team.

e. Cottage Industry

There is a way to greatly increase output without actually hiring employees to come and work in your workshop. You can farm out work to people who produce, usually part time, in their own homes. Many production crafts lend themselves particularly well to this "cottage industry" approach. There are many people who want to work part time at home, doing something they like. Starting a business wouldn't interest them, but they would welcome the opportunity to earn some extra cash doing pleasant work in their spare time.

The cottage industry approach has a number of advantages. If you do not control the hours and conditions of labor of the people who produce for you, so that they are not legally your employees, you are not involved with the mass of rules and regulations pertaining to employees. Your overhead costs are much less with a cottage system. You do not need to invest as much money in building, tools, and equipment as you would if you had employees working with your tools under your own roof.

However, there are limitations to the cottage industry approach. It generally works best where the craft skills required are readily available in the community so extensive training is not required. If, for example, there is a strong tradition of quiltmaking in an area, these skills could be used either directly in a quiltmaking operation or in making related products, such as patchwork clothing. However, there are numerous successful cottage industries where the workers are first trained in the employer's workshop before they start producing at home.

You have much less control over the quantity of output with this type of operation. If the home producer is bound by formal agreement to produce certain quantities or to work certain hours, the tax department may want to consider him or her an employee and you will in effect lose many of the advantages of a cottage industry. While you may not have a formal, written agreement, it is possible for you to have an understanding with the person producing at home so it is mutually understood that a certain amount of work will be produced. However, there are some gray areas here. Before getting too deeply involved with a cottage industry, you should first check, or ask your lawyer to check, whether there are any state or provincial laws which might affect your relationship with the home producers.

Quality control also requires special attention in a cottage industry situation. If work is being produced in your workshop, you can detect mistakes quickly and avoid having a lot of rejects or seconds produced. An outworker may produce a week's work or more before faults are discovered. There is no infallible system to prevent this from happening, but the risk can be reduced greatly by making sure that your home producers are conscientious, careful workers to begin with, by giving them proper training, and by having a system of quality control checks on all work as soon as it is received.

There is also some risk in the cottage industry approach that your designs or production techniques will be copied and used to produce work that is sold to someone else or sold directly by the worker. The chances of this happening can be reduced if you are careful to select honest, reliable people and you know their motivation in wanting to work at home.

It is of course possible to combine a cottage industry system with one where you have employees who come in to work. Some makers of production crafts have all their more complex pieces done in the workshop and put the simpler, straightforward work out.

Chapter 17

SOME TIPS FOR CONTINUED SUCCESS

a. Make Your Own Decisions

How big do you want your business to be? Do you want to hire people to work for you? These are questions involving major decisions that shape the future of your business. In the daily running of your business, there are many other decisions you will have to make. Is the Sam Slick Gift Shop in the town of Haliburton a good credit risk? Should you use that new dye the salesperson said was so good? Which of the two sewing machines you've looked at is the better buy?

Decision making is not just something that you'll have to do at crucial points in your business career. It is part of the day-to-day running of your business. Most decisions are basically simple. You add up all the pros and cons for each possible course of action and choose the best one.

This works in most cases. But what if you have looked thoroughly at all the advantages and disadvantages of alternative A and all the advantages and disadvantages of B and neither emerges clearly as the better choice? The reasons for selecting A may be just as good as the reasons for selecting B.

There is a natural tendency in such situations to want to do nothing at all or to procrastinate as long as possible. You should resist this tendency at all costs. If you are trying to decide which of two apparently good opportunities is better, procrastination could well cause you to miss both of them.

If, after weighing up all the possibilities in a given situation, no clear choice emerges and you are unable to make a decision based on external, objective factors, you must then use your intuition, your gut feelings, your natural instincts, or whatever you want to call it.

Some business people will say that they make all their decisions according to their feelings. Don't believe them. Most successful business moves depend on rational calculation. Still, when all is said and done, there is usually room for a measure of feeling or intuition in many decisions.

As a business person, you are a decision maker. It's not always easy, but you must learn to accept the role and avoid shying away from decisions — especially the difficult ones in which clear choices don't appear to exist.

SOME BUSINESS PEOPLE WILL SAY THAT THEY MAKE ALL THEIR DECISIONS ACCORDING TO THEIR FEELINGS. DON'T BELIEVE THEM.

b. When You Need Help, Ask for It

Don't forget to ask for help if you need it. Whether you are trying to solve a technical problem, set up a marketing system, locate a supplier, or tackle any of a hundred and one problems, there are others in the same boat as you. Use the resources of your local, national, or regional crafts organization; seek advice from other craftspeople, explore your public library, or search the Internet.

In the final analysis, you must make your own decision. Before you do so, however, get the best possible information you can. Never be afraid to ask a question or even to ask a favor. Most people are flattered when you seek their help and they will do their best to oblige you.

Librarians can be especially helpful. After all, it's part of their job. You can get an immense amount of information from your public library on many craft subjects. Books on specific crafts can provide the answers to technical questions such as how to fasten two pieces of metal together, how to achieve a certain finish on the outside of your pots, or what kind of preservative to use on your woodwork. You can locate the names and addresses of suppliers of raw materials or tools and equipment using the industrial and commercial directories that every good library has in its reference section. If you don't find what you want, ask a librarian.

Certain kinds of information may be found more easily and quickly on the Internet than by using other methods. Locating products made by major companies, for example, or finding possible outlets for your work in another part of the country can be relatively simple using the Net. If you don't have Internet access on your own computer or you don't have a computer, you can use the Internet access available at a public library to search for craft-related information.

c. Be Thoroughly Professional

To be successful in your craft business, you must be thoroughly professional. Accept nothing less than the highest standards in your work. Never cut corners to produce work by a certain deadline. Plan ahead as far as possible and allow yourself sufficient time to fill the orders you take. Don't take on more work than you can handle. The goodwill of your customers is one of your most valuable possessions. Don't jeopardize it by being late in delivering or by shipping work that is substandard.

d. Look After Details

A lot of the work of running a small business involves organization: organizing your time, planning your work, and planning your time off. If you adopt the attitude that only the big decisions are important and the little details will look after themselves, you're likely to end up a failure. Success in business depends on your ability to look after the details. On the other hand, don't become so bogged down in details that you can't see any longer where you are going.

e. Know When to Delegate

In the beginning of your business career you have to do everything yourself. You may build your own workshop, make all your products, get all the orders for your work, wrap your products, ship them to the customers, clean the floor, do the books, and so on. Later on, as your business grows, you may have people working for you and you can concentrate your energies where they are best used in your business.

If this is to work properly, you must be able to delegate work to others. This is one of the hardest things for many craftspeople to do.

There is a tendency to believe that only you can do the job right. In our business, we had to "educate" ourselves to accept the fact that others could actually be trained to produce our toys and turn them out as well as we could. Once we made this miraculous discovery, we were able to concentrate our own efforts on design, marketing, and quality control to make an even better product.

NO MATTER HOW FAR YOU GO IN YOUR CRAFT BUSINESS, THERE IS ALWAYS MORE TO LEARN ABOUT YOUR CRAFT AND ABOUT BUSINESS.

If you expand your business and hire people to work for you, your success will depend upon your ability to train and motivate your employees. To do this properly, you must have control at all times over costs and over the quality of your products. No matter how big your business grows, you must never let anything out of your workshop unless it is worthy of your own high professional standards. You can and must delegate work to others, but the ultimate responsibility for everything rests in your hands.

f. Never Stop Learning

No matter how far you go in your craft business, there is always more to learn about your craft and about business. You can learn from people, from books, and from experimenting on your own. A useful habit is to carry a small notebook with you and to jot down ideas as they occur to you. Be constantly on the lookout for new product ideas, new techniques, and new materials that you can use. Whenever you travel, look into craft and gift shops and check products and prices. Frequently, you'll see a product being sold in another part of the country that you can make or modify. Sometimes one of your customers may have a suggestion that you can turn into a money-making product.

Keep your eyes open for new market opportunities. The craft field is so incredibly flexible that it would be pointless to try to list all possible market opportunities. One craftsperson I know is making all kinds of money producing custom furniture for institutions and offices. Another is doing a healthy business supplying props for store windows. There are plenty of opportunities out there if you are prepared to use your imagination and put in a little hard work.

g. Your Leisure Time

Plan your time off wisely. If you are your own boss, you can also be your own worst enemy, subject to the mercy of your own whims and caprices. You can spend a lot of time goofing off or go to the opposite extreme and work yourself to death.

There are critical times in the life of every business when extraordinary effort and longer-than-average hours are called for. But if you find yourself permanently on a treadmill, you are doing something wrong. Perhaps you need to hire an assistant, get someone part time to do the bookkeeping or reorganize your work schedule. A well-run craft business should leave you sufficient time to enjoy other aspects of life.

A craft business does provide the opportunity to do away with the sharp distinction between work and play. For many people, work is an unpleasant necessity they want to get over with as quickly as possible so that they can begin "living." If you are working at something you like, you can abolish this distinction and achieve true contentment, enjoying both your work and your time off.

Even if you are in this fortunate position, don't forget to take time off. You may love your work, but you still need holidays at regular intervals. You need to renew your energies, to rest your mind and body, and to share other aspects of human experience. Also, and very important, there is your family to consider. If they're not happy and contented, you won't be, and if you're not reasonably happy, life is not worthwhile no matter how much money you are making.

Look at your craft business as a profession that provides you with some rather unique lifestyle advantages. It can bring you a good income doing something you like as well as a good measure of leisure time if you organize it properly. The chapter on production advocated controlling the size of your inventory with several factors in mind. I suggested keeping some extra inventory ready so you could handle orders during the peak season when you were busy invoicing and selling and unable to devote very much time to production.

In our production craft business, we used to build our inventory up so that we could take a good long summer vacation and go sailing. A lot of orders came in during the summer tourist season, so we would build up a large inventory in the early spring. During the summer, we went to the workshop one or two days a week to pack and ship the orders and do the paperwork. It cost us a little extra to build up our inventory so high in the spring, but it was worth it for the extra leisure time it made possible during the warm summer months.

There are plenty of ways you can vary your working hours to suit your own particular lifestyle. You may choose to work on the weekends and take a couple of days off in the middle of the week to escape the weekend crowds. Or you may prefer to work all summer and take your vacation at the end of the season when the tourist rush is over.

The key to a high return from your craft business is to choose the mix of salary, profit, and leisure that brings you the highest degree of satisfaction. If you are facing a difficult period, you may have to work harder and put in more hours than usual, but once your business is established, you have the opportunity to take your rewards in the form of increased leisure as well as profits.

h. Licensing

Some very interesting new possibilities for craftspeople have emerged in connection with the recent tremendous popularity of licensed products. The importance of licensed products has grown astronomically in the United States and Canada in the past decade.

Traditionally, licensing has attracted a high degree of attention in the areas of toys, children's wear, and juvenile merchandise. In recent years, it has spread to many other areas, including clothing of all kinds, housewares, pottery, and jewelry.

Until quite recently, most successful licensed products came from movies, cartoons, and television. Today, more and more licensed products do not spring from the entertainment industry but from other origins. Some are the result of a drawing board concept that is developed and marketed according to a calculated licensing program. Others have their origins in the craft world, and have been made into huge commercial successes by large North American manufacturers with computerized assembly lines producing "individualized, one-of-a-kind" products.

Some craftspeople are appalled by the idea of using a computerized assembly line to produce simulated handcrafts. They argue that such products can never attain the quality of real handcrafted goods. Others see the new production techniques as a step into the post-industrial society of the future, an opportunity to make high-quality, unique products available to a wide market.

There is no argument over the tremendous appeal of handcrafted products today. In this context, licensing offers the craftsperson a means of making his or her work widely available. If a craftsperson has designed and made a highly successful product that appears to have a wide market appeal — far beyond the limits of an individual's production capacity — it may be possible to license others to produce the product in return for a royalty fee based on a certain percentage of sales.

While the returns from licensing can be highly lucrative, the field is fraught with risks. There are huge promotional, advertising, and legal expenses. The growth of the licensing field has spawned a new type of professional: the licensing agent. This individual or company acts as a go-between for manufacturers and the licenser. If you think that your handcrafted product has licensing possibilities, it may be worth talking to a licensing agent. Two trade magazines, *The Licensing Letter* and the *Merchandising Reporter*, can provide more information on licensing.

i. Protecting Your Craft Designs

What if some "unlicensed" person, that is, some person not authorized by you, uses your designs? Not only do you receive nothing in return for such unauthorized use, you may also lose some of the profits from the lost sales of your own products. Is there anything you can do to prevent this?

There are laws in both Canada and the United States that provide protection against the unauthorized use of an industrial design. The subject of design protection is highly complex and can only be touched on briefly here. To protect a particular design, you can register the design (not to be confused with a patent or a copyright, both of which are quite different) under industrial design legislation, which is in effect in both Canada and the United States.

At first glance this might seem to be a simple and foolproof way of establishing one's exclusive claim to a particular design. In practice, the situation is far from simple. There is the necessity of policing the design; that is, watching out for violations and prosecuting offenders or settling with them out of court, which (needless to say) can be extremely expensive and time consuming.

Most of the legal actions involving design infringement are undertaken by large corporations. Individual craftspeople and small craft companies can rarely afford the high costs of such litigation.

The very fact that you have registered your design may have a deterrent effect on many would-be pirates, but the actual amount of protection that you have is debatable because it is sometimes possible for another person to simply alter your design slightly and then quite legitimately use it in his or her own product.

It is possible to protect a design in a somewhat limited and indirect way by the use of a trademark. You register a name — "Explosions!!" or "Jewelry by Alfonso" or whatever fancy name you can come up with that is not already in use by someone else — and use that name on your products. This means, in effect, that while competitors may still copy your designs, they cannot put your trademark on their products. Thus, your design is "protected" to the extent that customers recognize and are loyal to your name or particular trademark. This, of course, depends to a great extent on customer recognition of your trademark and the loyalty of your customers.

If you feel it is worthwhile to register your designs, you should definitely get the advice of a legal professional who specializes in this subject.

THE VERY FACT THAT YOU HAVE REGISTERED YOUR DESIGN MAY HAVE A DETERRENT EFFECT ON MANY WOULD-BE PIRATES.

j.   Using the Designs of Others

Suppose you come across a design by another person or company that you wish to copy and use in your own work. If the design is protected — that is, if it is registered as a design patent (in the u.s.) or as an industrial design (in Canada) — you can use it legally only with the owner's permission. If you use it without permission, you leave yourself open to legal action, including the possibility of being sued for damages. This can happen even if, by chance, you come up with a design of your own that, unknown to you, is already protected under patent law.

If you wish to copy someone else's design, it is advisable to contact the owner or publisher to determine whether the design is protected. Alternatively, you could contact the appropriate authorities (the Patent Office in the u.s. or the Commissioner of Patents in Canada) if you want to verify whether a particular design is protected. If a design is registered, the owner may be willing to grant permission to make copies upon payment of a fee, or it may be possible for you to change the design in order for it to be considered different. Some craftspeople copy commercial designs without bothering to obtain the owners' permission. In some cases, these small-scale "pirates" can get away with illegal copying. But if you are tempted to take that route, think again. Your professional reputation may suffer if it is known that you make frequent use (whether legally or otherwise) of commercial designs. Sometimes a craftsperson is excluded from membership in craft councils or participation in juried craft shows on the grounds that his or her work makes too much use of commercial designs. In the long run, this can affect them directly in their pocketbooks when they find themselves cut off from the customary exchange of information and ideas that are shared among their peers.

None of this discussion is meant to imply that you must never copy someone else's design. Indeed, many craftspeople make use of the designs of others, whether traditional or contemporary. Not every craftsperson is a good designer, and from an aesthetic as well as a business point of view, it is often better to use a good design by someone else than a poor one of your own creation.

Some of the best craftspeople hire free-lance designers to create their designs. Others take an existing design and play with it, experimenting until they come up with something sufficiently different to constitute a new design. Still others draw on the vast stock of traditional designs, many of which have originated in past centuries and are no longer the property of any individual or company.

If you are in doubt about a particular aspect of design protection as it applies to your work, it is advisable to seek the advice of a lawyer who specializes in the area of intellectual property (patents, copyright, and trademarks).

Appendix 1

DIRECTORIES AND GUIDES

a. Retail Craft Show Guides

Sunshine Artist Magazine
3210 Dade Ave.
Orlando, FL 32804

This publication provides lists of U.S. art and craft shows. The magazine has set up and maintains a searchable database on the World Wide Web (searchable by date, city, state, or region) of art and craft shows at <www.artandcraftshows.net>. You can also visit the magazine's Web site at <www.sunshineartist.com>.

The Crafts Report
100 Rogers Rd.
Wilmington, Delaware 19801-5041

The Crafts Report, established in 1975, is a monthly business magazine for the professional craftsperson. The magazine has a searchable database (searchable by date, state, show category, type of craft) of craft shows on its Web site at <www.craftsreport.com>.

Artist's and Graphic Designer's Market
Writer's Digest Books
1507 Dana Avenue
Cincinnati, Ohio 45207

This publication lists many galleries that deal in crafts, and features articles about the business of art. It also lists companies that buy some craft designs.

b. Wholesale Show Guides

National Craft Association
2012 E. Ridge Rd., Suite 120
Rochester, NY 14622-2434
Phone: (585) 266-5472,
Fax: (585) 785-3231
www.craftassoc.com

For a list of wholesale resources see the Association's Web page:

www.craftassoc.com/00003a.html

Trade Show News Network
PO Box 6511
Holliston, MA 01746
info@tsnn.com

For a searchable database of wholesale trade shows, including art and craft shows see <www.tsnn.com>.

c. Directory of Sales Representatives

Manufacturers' Agents National Association
Directory of Members
One Spectrum Pointe, Suite 150
Lake Forest, CA 92630
Phone: (949) 859-4040
Toll Free: 1-877-MANA-PRO (626-2776)
Fax: (949) 855-2973
www.manaonline.org
E-mail: MANA@MANAonline.org

d. Directory of Local, Provincial and State Development Agencies

Economic Development Directory
One Rustic Ridge, D-27
Little Falls, NJ 07424
Phone: 973-812-1944
E-mail: pokeefe@ecodevdirectory.com

The Economic Development Directory is located at <www.ecodevdi-rectory.com>. This site is a directory of economic development Web sites worldwide. In the US and Canada, listings in each state and province are further divided geographically so a user can find regional and even local agencies. If you do not have a computer with Internet access, it is worthwhile using the Internet services of your local library to view this Web site.

CRAFT ORGANIZATIONS/ AGENCIES

It is not feasible in a book of this size to provide a comprehensive list of all craft organizations and agencies in the US and Canada. The larger organizations are listed in telephone directories. Smaller local craft organizations can often be located by contacting the state and/or provincial groups listed below.

Please note that while all contact information in the lists below was current at the time of writing, entries are subject to change, which is beyond the control of the author or publisher.

a. United States

NATIONAL

American Art Pottery Association
PO Box 834
Westport, MA 02790-0697
www.amartpot.org
E-mail: AmArtPotAssn@aol.com

American Association of Woodturners
222 Landmark Center
St. Paul, MN 55102
Phone: (651) 484-9094   Fax:(651) 484-1724
www.woodturner.org
E-mail: woodturner@gwest.net

American Bladesmith Society Inc.
PO Box 1481
Cypress, TX 77410-1481
www.americanbladesmith.com

American Ceramics Society
PO Box 6136
Westerville, OH 43086-6136
Phone: (614) 890-4700   Fax: (614) 899-6109
www.ceramics.org
E-mail: info@ceramics.org

American Council for the Arts
1 E. 53rd St., 2nd Floor
New York, NY 10022
Phone: (212) 223-2787
www.artsusa.org

American Craft Council
72 Spring St.
New York, NY 10012-4019
Phone: (212) 274-0630
www.craftcouncil.org
E-mail: mmcghee@craftcouncil.org

American Needlepoint Guild, Inc.
7600 Terrace Ave., Suite 203
Middleton, WI 53562
Phone: (608) 836-1503
www.needlepoint.org
E-mail:membership@needlepoint.org

American Quilter's Society
PO Box 3290
Paducah, KY 42002-3290
Phone: (270) 898-7903   Fax: (270) 898-1173
www.americanquilter.com
E-mail:info@aqsquilt.com

Art Alliance for Contemporary Glass
PO Box 7022
Evanston, IL 60201
Phone: (847) 869-2018
www.contempglass.org
E-mail: admin@contempglass.org

Artist-Blacksmith's Association of North America
PO Box 816
Farmington, GA 30638
www.abana.org

Center for Bead Research
Note: This site is for research purposes only. They are no longer processing subscriptions or taking memberships.
www.thebeadsite.com

Center for the Study of Beadwork
PO Box 13719
Portland, OR 97213
Phone: (503) 655-3078
www.europa.com/~alice

Hobby & Craft Association
319 E. 54th St.
Elmwood Park, NJ 07407
Phone: (201) 794-1133   Fax: (201) 797-0657
www.hobby.org
E-mail: info@craftandhobby.org

Craft Yarn Council of America
PO Box 9
Gastonia, NC 28053
Phone: (704) 824-7838
www.craftyarncouncil.com
E-mail: cycainfo@aol.com

The Crafts Center
8601 Georgia Ave., Suite 800
Washington, DC 20910
Phone: (301) 587-4700   Fax: (301) 587-7393
www.craftscenter.org
E-mail: craftscenter@chfhq.com

Creative Glass Center of America (CGCA)
Wheaton Village
1501 Glasstown Rd.
Millville, NJ 08332-1566
Phone: (609) 825-6800   Fax: (609) 825-2410
www.wheatonvillage.org/creativeglasscenteramerica
E-mail: cgca@wheatonvillage.org

The Embroiderers' Guild of America, Inc.
335 West Broadway, Suite 100
Louisville, KY 40202
Phone: (502) 589-6956   Fax: (502) 584-7900
www.egausa.org
E-mail: egahq@egausa.org

The Enamelist Society
6105 Bay Hill Circle
Jamesville, NY 13078
www.enamelistsociety.com
E-mail: averill@enamelist.com

Friends of Fiber Art International
PO Box 468
Western Springs, IL 60558

The Furniture Society
PO Box 18
Free Union, VA 22940
Phone: (434) 973-1488   Fax: (434) 973-0336
www.furnituresociety.org
E-mail: mail@furnituresociety.org

Glass Art Society
1305 Fourth Ave., Suite 711
Seattle, WA 98101
Phone: (206) 382-1305   Fax: (206) 382-2630
www.glassart.org
E-mail: info@glassart.org

Guild of American Papercutters
PO Box 651351
Sterling, PA 20165
www.papercutters.org
E-mail: brittatwo@yahoo.com

Hand Papermaking
PO Box 77027
Washington, DC 20013-7027
Phone: (301) 220-2393
Toll free: (800) 821-6604   Fax: (301) 220-2394
www.handpapermaking.org
E-mail: info@handpapermaking.org

James Renwick Alliance
4405 East-West Highway, Suite 510
Bethesda, MD 20814
Phone: (301) 907-3888   Fax: (301) 907-3855
www.jra.org
E-mail: jraoffice@jra.org

The Knitting Guild
PO Box 3388
Zanesville, OH 43702-3388
Phone: (740) 452-4541   Fax: (740) 452-2552
www.tkga.com
E-mail: tkga@tkga.com

Marquetry Society of America
99 Wintergreen Way
Rochester, NY 14618
Phone: (716) 271-3566
E-mail: halhelsen@aol.com

National Assembly of State Arts Agencies
1029 Vermont Ave. NW, 2nd Floor
Washington, DC 20005
Phone: (202) 347-6352   Fax: (202) 737-0526
www.nasaa-arts.org
E-mail: nasaa@nasaa-arts.org

National Institute of American Doll Artists
www.niada.org
E-mail: niada@niada.org

National Association of Independent Artists
www.naia-artists.org
E-mail: ArdathPrendergast@naia-artists.org

National Basketry Organization, Inc.
11730 Mountain Park Rd.
Roswell, GA 30075
Phone: (770) 641-9208
www.nationalbasketry.org
E-mail: contact@nationalbasketry.org

National Craft Association
2012 E. Ridge Rd., Suite 120
Rochester, NY 14622-2434
Phone: (585) 266-5472
Toll free: (800) 715-9594   Fax: (585) 785-3231
www.craftassoc.com
E-mail: nca@craftassoc.com

National Guild of Decoupeurs
c/o Marion D. Peer
1017 Pucker St.
Stowe, VT 05672
Phone: (802) 253-3903
www.decoupage.org
E-mail: mdpeer@aol.com

National Polymer Clay Guild
1350 Beverly Rd., Suite 115-345
McLean, VA 22101
www.npcg.org

The National Quilting Association
PO Box 12190
Columbus, OH 43212
Phone: (614) 488-8520   Fax: (614) 488-8521
www.nqaquilts.org
E-mail: nqaquilts@sbcglobal.net

National Wood Carvers Association
PO Box 43218
Cincinnati, OH 45243
www.chipchats.org
E-mail: nwca@chipchats.org

Society of American Silversmiths
PO Box 72839
Providence, RI 02907
Phone: (401) 461-6840
Fax: (401) 461-6841
www.silversmithing.com
E-mail: sas@silversmithing.com

Society of Arts and Crafts
175 Newbury St.
Boston, MA 02116
Phone: (617) 266-1810
www.societyofcrafts.org
E-mail: bgerstein@societyofcrafts.org

Society of Craft Designers
PO Box 3388
Zanesville, OH 43702-3388
Phone: (740) 452-4541   Fax: (740) 452-2552
www.craftdesigners.org
E-mail: scd@offinger.com

Studio Art Quilt Associates
PO Box 572
Storrs, CT 06268
Phone: (860) 487-4198   Fax: (860) 487-4198
www.saqa.com
E-mail: director@saqa.com

The Society of North American Goldsmiths
1300 Iroquis Ave., Suite 160
Naperville, IL 60563-8063
Phone: (630) 778-6385   Fax: (630) 416-3333
www.snagmetalsmith.org
E-mail: info@snagmetalsmith.org

Stained Glass Association of America
10009 E. 62nd St.
Raytown, MO 64133
Toll free: (800) 438-9581
www.stainedglass.org
E-mail: sgaa@kcnet.com

Surface Design Association
PO Box 360
Sebastopol, CA 95473-0360
Phone: (707) 829-3110   Fax: (707) 829-3285
www.surfacedesign.org
E-mail: surfacedesign@mail.com

Wood Turning Center
501 Vine St.
Philadelphia, PA 19106
Phone: (215) 923-8000   Fax (215) 923-4403
www.woodturningcenter.org
E-mail: info@woodturningcenter.org

ALABAMA
Alabama Crafts Council
Kentucky Center
503 Main Ave.
Northport, AL 36130
Phone: (205) 333-1252

Alabama State Council on the Arts
201 Monroe St.
Montgomery, AL 36130-1800
Phone: (334) 242-4076   Fax: (334) 240-3269
www.arts.state.al.us
E-mail: staff@arts.alabama.gov

Birmingham Art Association
PO Box 425
1804 3rd Ave. N.
Birmingham, AL 35201
Phone: (205) 324-9127
www.birminghamartassociation.org
E-mail: mail@birminghamartassociation.org

ALASKA
Alaska State Council on the Arts
411 W. 4th Ave., Suite 1E
Anchorage, AK 99501-2343
Phone: (907) 269-6610
Toll free: (888) 278-7424   Fax: (907) 269-6601
www.edu.state.ak.us/aksca
E-mail: info@aksca.org

ARIZONA
Arizona Commission on the Arts
417 W. Roosevelt St.
Phoenix, AZ 85003
Phone: (602) 255-5882   Fax: (602) 256-0282
www.arizonaarts.org
E-mail: general@arizonaarts.org

Arizona Designer Craftsmen
1669 N. 106th Way
Scottsdale, AZ 85255
www.intrec.com/adc

Artlink
PO Box 3426
Phoenix, AZ 85030
Phone: (602) 256-7539   Fax: (602) 256-4577
www.artlinkpheonix.com
E-mail: info@artlinkpheonix.com

Coconino Center for the Arts
PO Box 296
2300 N. Fort Valley Rd., Route 180
Flagstaff, AZ 86001
Phone: (928) 779-2300
www.culturalpartners.org

Mountain Artists Guild
228 N. Alarcon
Prescott, AZ 86301
Phone: (928) 445-2510   Fax: (928) 776-4861
www.mountainartistguild.org
E-mail: mag@northlink.com

ARKANSAS
Arkansas Arts Council
1500 Tower Bldg.
323 Center St.
Little Rock, AR 72201
Phone: (501) 324-9766   Fax: (501) 324-9207
www.arkansasarts.com
E-mail: info@arkansasarts.com

Arkansas Crafts Guild
PO Box 800
104 E. Main St.
Mountain View, AR 72560
Phone: (870) 269-3897
www.arkansascraftguild.org
E-mail: arkcrafguild@mvtel.net

Avoca Arts Council
PO Box 69
Avoca, AR 72711

Malvern Arts/Crafts
PO Box 1414
Malvern, AR 72104

Ozarks Arts and Crafts Association
11036 High Sky Inn Rd.
Hindsville, AR 72738
Phone: (501) 789-5398   Fax: (501) 789-2215
www.wareagle.com
E-mail: wareagle@specent.com

Village Art Club
PO Box 5009
Bella Vista, AR 72714
Phone: (479) 855-2064
www.villageartclub.org
E-mail: artclub@ipa.net

Western Arkansas Arts & Crafts Association
PO Box 334
Wickes, AR 71973

CALIFORNIA
Association of Clay and Glass Artists of California (ACGA)
1045 Center St.
San Carlos, CA 94070
Phone: (925) 254-8457
www.acga.net
E-mail: anntesta@aol.com

California Arts Council
1300 I St., Suite 930
Sacramento, CA 95814
Phone: (916) 322-6555
Toll free: (800) 201-6201   Fax: (916) 322-6575
www.cac.ca.gov

Cerritos Art Association
PO Box 3608
Cerritos, CA 90703
www.cerritosart.com

La Quinta Arts Foundation
PO Box 777
La Quinta, CA 92247
Phone: (760) 564-1244   Fax: (760) 564-6884
www.la-quinta-arts-found.org
E-mail: christi@lqaf.com

Leathercraft Guild
6252 Najvaho Rd.
Westminster, CA 92683-2038
E-mail: leather-guild@juno.com

Mammoth Art Guild
PO Box 56
Mammoth Lakes, CA 93546
Phone: (760) 873-7242
www.mammothartguild.com

Metal Arts Society of Southern California (MASSC)
PO Box 1014
El Toro, CA 92609
www.massconline.com
E-mail: info@massconline.com

Plumas County Arts Commission
PO Box 618
Quincy, CA 95971
Phone: (530) 283-3402   Fax: (530) 283-1168
www.plumasarts.com

Santee Arts Council
PO Box 710253
Santee, CA 92072

Western States Craft & Hobby Association
PO Box 1007
Huntington Beach, CA 92647
Phone: (310) 430-6038

COLORADO

Arvada Center for the Arts
Phone: (720) 898-7210
www.arvadacenter.org

Evergreen Artists Association
PO Box 1511
Evergreen, CO 80437
Phone: (303) 679-1609
www.evergreenartists.org
E-mail: info@evergreenartists.org

Fine Arts Guild
PO Box 1165
Estes Park, CO 80517
Phone: (970) 586-9203
www.fineartsguild.org
E-mail: cwood@peakpeak.com

Western States Arts Federation
1743 Wazee St., Suite 300
Denver, CO 80202
Phone: (303) 629-1166
Toll free: (888) 562-7232   Fax: (303) 629-9717
www.westaf.org
E-mail: staff@westaf.org

CONNECTICUT

Brookfield Craft Center
PO Box 122
Brookfield, CT 06804
Phone: (203) 775-4526   Fax: (203) 740-7815
www.brookfieldcraftcenter.org
E-mail: info@brookfieldcraftcenter.org

Connecticut Commission on the Arts
One Financial Plaza, 755 Main St.
Hartford, CT 06103
Phone: (860) 256-2800   Fax: (860) 256-2811
www.ctarts.org
E-mail: artsinfo@ctarts.org

Creative Arts Workshop
80 Audubon St.
New Haven, CT 06510
Phone: (203) 562-4927   Fax: (203) 562-2329
www.creativeartsworkshop.org

Glastonbury Art Guild
1396 Hebron Ave.
Glastonbury, CT 06033
Phone: (860) 659-1196   Fax: (860) 633-4301
www.glastonburyartguild.com
E-mail: glast.art.guild@sbcglobal.net

Society for Connecticut Crafts
PO Box 615
Hartford, CT 06142
Phone: (203) 265-2365

DELAWARE

Delaware Center for the Contemporary Arts (DCCA)
200 S. Madison St.
Wilmington, DE 19801
Phone: (302) 656-6466   Fax: (302) 656-6944
www.thedcca.org
E-mail: info@thedcca.org

Delaware State Arts Council
Delaware Division of the Arts
Carvel State Office Bldg.
820 N. French St.
Wilmington, DE 19801
Phone: (302) 577-8278
www.artsdel.org

Rehoboth Art League
12 Dodds Lane
Rehoboth Beach, DE 19971
Phone: (302) 227-8408   Fax: (302) 227-4121
www.rehobothartleague.org

FLORIDA

Florida Craftsmen, Inc.
501 Central Ave.
St. Petersburg, FL 33701-3703
Phone: (727) 821-7391   Fax: (727) 822-4294
www.floridacraftsmen.net
Email: info@floridacraftsmen.net

Division of Cultural Affairs
1001 DeSoto Park Dr.
Tallahassee, FL 32301
Phone: (850) 245-6470   Fax: (850) 245-6497
www.florida-arts.org
E-mail: info@florida-arts.org

GEORGIA

Browns Crossing Craftsmen
400 Browns Crossing Rd. NW
Milledgeville, GA 31061

Chattahoochee Handweavers Guild
PO Box 889244
Atlanta, GA 30356
www.chgweb.com
E-mail: admin@chgweb.com

Crochet Association International
PO Box 131
Dallas, GA 30132
Phone: (770) 445-7137

Georgia Council for the Arts
260 14th St. NW, Suite 401
Atlanta, GA 30318-5730
Phone: (404) 685-2787   Fax: (404) 685-2788
www.gaarts.org
E-mail: gaarts@gaarts.org

Southern Arts Federation (SAF)
1401 Peachtree St. NW, Suite 808
Atlanta, GA 30309-7603
Phone: (404) 874-7244   Fax: (404) 873-2148
www.southarts.org

HAWAII

State Foundation on Culture & the Arts
250 S. Hotel St., 2nd Floor
Honolulu, HI 96813
Phone: (808) 586-0300   Fax: (808) 586-0308
www.state.hi.us/sfca
E-mail: ken.hamilton@hawaii.gov/sfca

IDAHO

Idaho Commission on the Arts
2410 N. Old Penitentiary Rd.
Boise, ID 83712
Phone: (208) 334-2119   Fax: (208) 334-2119
www.state.id.us/arts

ILLINOIS

Illinois Artisans Program
James R. Thompson Center
100 W. Randolph, Suite 4-300
Chicago, IL 60601
Phone: (312) 814-4945   Fax: (312) 814-1794
www.museum.state.il.us

American Society of Artists
PO Box 1326
Palatine, IL 60078
Phone: (312) 751-2500
www.americansocietyofartists.com
E-mail: asoa@webtv.net

Chicago Artists' Coalition (CAC)
11 E. Hubbard
Chicago, IL 60611
Phone: (312) 670-2060   Fax: (312) 670-2521
www.caconline.org
E-mail: webmaster@caconline.org

Craft Retailers Marketing Council
1506 Sherman Dr.
Evanston, IL 60201
Phone: (708)258-6105

Illinois Arts Council
James R. Thompson Center
100 W. Randolph, Suite 10-500
Chicago, IL 60601
Phone: (312) 814-6750   Fax: (312) 814-1471
www.state.il.us/agency/iac
E-mail: info@arts.state.il.us

INDIANA

Indiana Arts Commission
150 W. Market St., Suite 618
Indianapolis, IN 46204-2741
Phone: (317) 232-1268   Fax: (317) 232-5595
www.in.gov/arts
E-mail: indianaartscommsion@iac.in.gov

Quilter's Hall of Fame
PO Box 681
Marion, IN 46952
Phone: (765)664-9333
www.quiltershalloffame.org
E-mail: quilters@comteck.com

Indiana Artist Craftsmen
323 Greyhound Pass
Carmel, IN 46032

IOWA

Craft Guild of Iowa City
815 Oakland
Iowa City, IA 52240
Phone: (319) 338-2151
E-mail: tjones@soli.inav.net

Iowa Arts Council
600 E. Locust
Des Moines, IA 50319-0290
Phone: (515) 281-6412   Fax: (515) 242-6498
www.iowaartscouncil.org

KANSAS

Kansas Artist-Craftsmen Association
PO Box 405
Morland, KS 67650-0405

Kansas Arts Commission (KAC)
700 SW Jackson, Suite 1004
Topeka, KS 66603-3758
Phone: (785) 296-3335   Fax: (785) 296-4989
http://arts.state.ks.us
E-mail: KAC@arts.state.ks.us

The Salina Arts and Humanities Commission
PO Box 2181
Salina, KS 67402-2181
Phone: (785) 309-5770   Fax: (785) 826-7444
www.salinaarts.com
E-mail: sahc@salina.org

KENTUCKY

Kentucky Museum of Art and Craft
715 W. Main St.
Louisville, KY 40202
Phone: (502) 589-0102   Fax: (502) 589-0154
www.kentuckycrafts.org

Kentucky Craft Marketing Program
Old Capitol Annex
300 W. Broadway
Frankfort, KY 40601
Phone: (502) 564-3757
Toll Free: (888) 592-7238   Fax: (502) 564-5696
www.kycraft.org
E-mail: kycraft@ky.gov

Kentucky Guild of Artists & Craftsmen
103 Parkway
Berea, KY 40403-9114
Phone: (859) 986-3192   Fax: (859) 985-9114
www.kyguild.org
E-mail: info@kyguild.org

LOUISIANA

Louisiana Division of the Arts
PO Box 44247
Baton Rouge, LA 70804
Phone: (225) 342-8180   Fax: (225) 342-8173
www.crt.state.la.us/arts
E-mail: arts@crt.state.la.us

MAINE

Maine Arts Commission
193 State St.
25 State House Station
Augusta, ME 04333
Phone: (207) 287-2360   Fax: (207) 287-2725
www.mainearts.com
E-mail: MaineArts.info@maine.gov

Maine Crafts Association
PO Box 8817
Portland, ME 04104
Phone: (207) 780-1807
wwww.mainecrafts.org
E-mail: info@mainecrafts.org

United Maine Craftsmen
16 Old Winthrop Rd., Suite 2
Manchester, ME 04351
Phone: (207) 621-2818   Fax: (207) 621-1945
www.mainecraftsmen.org
E-mail: umc@mainecraftsmen.org

MARYLAND

Maryland State Arts Council
175 W. Ostend St., Suite E
Baltimore, MD 21230
Phone: (410) 767-6555   Fax: (410) 333-4519
www.msac.org
E-mail: msac@msac.org

Mid-Atlantic Arts Foundation
201 N. Charles St., Suite 401
Baltimore, MD 21201
Phone: (410) 539-6656   Fax: (410) 837-5517
www.midatlanticarts.org
E-mail: maaf@midatlanticarts.org

MASSACHUSETTS
New England Foundation for the Arts
145 Tremont St., 7th Floor
Boston, MA 02111
Phone: (617) 951-0010
www.nefa.org
E-mail: info@nefa.org

MICHIGAN
Michigan Council for Arts & Cultural Affairs
PO Box 30705
702 W. Kalamazoo
Lansing, MI 48909
Phone: (517) 241-4011   Fax: (313) 241-3979
www.michigan.gov
E-mail: artsinfo@michigan.gov

Michigan Guild of Artists & Artisans
Lock Box 8178
Ann Arbor, MI 48107
Phone: (734) 662-3382
www.michiganguild.org
E-mail: guild@michiganguild.org

MINNESOTA
Arts Midwest
2908 Hennepin Ave., Suite 200
Minneapolis, MN 55408-1954
Phone: (612) 341-0755   Fax: (612) 341-0902
www.artsmidwest.org
E-mail: general@artsmidwest.org

Minnesota Crafts Council
528 Hennepin Ave., Suite 216
Minneapolis, MN 55403-1896
Phone: (612) 333-7789
Toll free: (888) 805-1068   Fax: (612) 204-0409
www.mncraft.org
E-mail: mncraft@mtn.org

Minnesota State Arts Board
Park Square Court
400 Sibley St., Suite 200
St. Paul, MN 55101-1928
Phone: (651) 215-1600
Toll free: (800) 866-2787   Fax: (651) 215-1602
www.arts.state.mn.us
E-mail: msab@state.mn.us

MISSISSIPPI
Mississippi Crafts Center
PO Box 69
Natchez Trace Parkway
Ridgeland, MS 39157
Phone: (601) 981-0019

Craftsmen's Guild of Mississippi
1150 Lakeland Dr.
Jackson, MS 39216
Phone: (601) 981-0019   Fax: (601) 981-0488
www.mscraftsmensguild.org
E-mail: mscraftsmen@aol.com

Mississippi Arts Commission
239 N. Lamar St., Suite 207
Jackson, MS 39201
Phone: (601) 359-6030   Fax: (601) 359-6008
www.arts.state.ms.us

MISSOURI
Mid-America Arts Alliance
912 Baltimore Ave., Suite 700
Kansas City, MO 64105
Phone: (816) 421-1388   Fax: (816) 421-3918
www.maaa.org
E-mail: info@maaa.org

Craft Alliance
6640 Delmar Blvd.
St. Louis, MO 63130
Phone: (314) 725-1151   Fax: (314) 725-2068
www.craftalliance.org
E-mail: info@craftalliance.org

Missouri Arts Council
Wainwright Office Complex
111 N. 7th St., Suite 105
St. Louis, MO 63101-2188
Phone: (314) 340-6845
Toll free: (866) 407-4752   Fax: (314) 340-7215
www.missouriartscouncil.org
E-mail: moarts@mail.state.mo.us

MONTANA
Montana Arts Council
PO Box 202201
Helena, MT 59620
Phone: (406) 444-6430   Fax: (406) 444-6548
www.art.state.mt.us
E-mail: mac@mt.gov

NEBRASKA
GROW Nebraska
PO Box 7
416 Central Ave.
Holbrook, NE 68948
Toll free: (888) 476-9632
www.growneb.com
E-mail: info@growneb.com

Nebraska HomeBased Business Association
PO Box 54
David City, NE 68632
Toll free: (800) 414-3906
Fax: (402) 367-4712
www.nhbba.org
E-mail: info@nhbba.org

NEVADA
Nevada Arts Council
716 N. Carson St., Suite A
Carson City, NV 89701
Phone: (775) 687-6680   Fax: (775) 687-6688
www.dmla.clan.lib.nv.us
E-mail: jcounsil@clan.lib.nv.us

NEW HAMPSHIRE
League of New Hampshire Craftsmen
205 N. Main St.
Concord, NH 03301-5080
Phone: (603) 224-3375   Fax: (603) 225-8452
www.nhcrafts.org
E-mail: nhleague@nhcrafts.org

New Hampshire State Council on the Arts
2½ Beacon St., 2nd Floor
Concord, NH 03301
Phone: (603) 271-2789   Fax: (603) 271-3584
www.state.nh.gov/nharts

NEW JERSEY
New Jersey Designer Craftsmen
65 Church St.
New Brunswick, NJ 08901-1242

Montclair Craft Guild
Dept. CR, PO Box 538
Glen Ridge, NJ 07028
Phone: (201) 783-4110   Fax: (973) 744-8689
E-mail:montclair_craft_guild@hotmail.com

New Jersey State Council on the Arts
PO Box 306
225 W. State St.
Trenton, NJ 08625-0306
Phone: (609) 292-6130   Fax: (609) 989-1140
www.njartscouncil.org
E-mail: njsca@arts.sos.state.nj.us

Peters Valley Craft Education Center
19 Kuhn Rd.
Layton, NJ 07851
Phone: (973) 948-5200   Fax: (973) 948-0011
www.pvcrafts.org
E-mail: pv@warick.net

NEW MEXICO
New Mexico Arts
Department of Cultural Affairs
PO Box 1450
Santa Fe, NM 87504
Phone: (505) 827-6490   Fax: (505) 827-6043
www.nmarts.org

Santa Fe Arts Commission
PO Box 909
Santa Fe, NM 87504
Phone: (505) 955-6707   Fax: (505) 955-6671
www.santafenm.gov
E-mail: artscommission@cisantafe.nh.us

Santa Fe Council for the Arts
PO Box 8921
Santa Fe, NM 87504
Phone: (505) 424-1878

Taos Center for the Arts
133 Paseo del Pueblo Norte
Taos, NM 87571
Phone: (505) 758-2052   Fax: (505) 751-3305
www.taoscenterforthearts.org

Southwest Association for Indian Arts
PO Box 969
Santa Fe, NM 87504
Phone: (505) 983-5220   Fax: (505) 983-7647
www.swaia.org
E-mail: info@swaia.org

NEW YORK
Empire State Crafts Alliance
329 Montgomery St.
Syracuse, NY 13202
Phone: (315) 472-4245

Long Island Craft Guild
www.licg.org
E-mail: info@licg.org

New York State Council on the Arts
175 Varick St.
New York, NY 10014
Phone: (212) 627-4455
www.nysca.org

Westchester Art Workshop
Westchester County Center
196 Central Ave.
White Plains, NY 10606
Phone: (914) 606-7500
North Carolina

Piedmont Craftsmen
601 N. Trade St.
Winston-Salem, NC 27101
Phone: (336) 725-1516   Fax: (336) 722-6038
www.piedmontcraftsmen.org
E-mail: info@piedmontcraftsmen.org

Carolina Designer Craftsmen
PO Box 2384
Raleigh, NC 27602
Phone: (919) 460-1551
www.carolinadesignercraftsmen.com
E-mail: info@carolinadesignercraftsmen.com

Southern Highland Handicraft Guild
Milepost 382
PO Box 9545
Asheville, NC 28815
Phone: (828) 298-7928   Fax: (828) 298-7962
www.southernhighlandguild.org
E-mail: info@southernhighlandguild.org

HandMade in America
PO Box 2089
Asheville, NC 28802
Phone: (828) 252-0121
www.handmadeinamerica.org
E-mail: info@handmadeinamerica.org

North Carolina Arts Council
Department of Cultural Resources
Raleigh, NC 27699-4632
Phone: (919) 733-2111   Fax: (919) 733-4834
www.ncarts.org
E-mail: ncarts@ncacmail.net

NORTH DAKOTA
North Dakota Council on the Arts
1600 E. Century Ave., Suite 6
Bismarck, ND 58503
Phone: (701) 328-7590   Fax: (701) 328-7595
www.state.nd.us/arts
E-mail: comserv@state.nd.us

OHIO
Ohio Arts and Crafts Guild
PO Box 3080
25 Walnut St.
Lexington, OH 44904
Phone: (419) 884-9622   Fax: (419) 884-9641
www.cg-tinsmith.com/oacg
E-mail: OHIOACG@aol.com

Ohio Designer Craftsmen
1665 W. 5th Ave.
Columbus, OH 43212
Phone: (614) 486-4402   Fax: (614) 486-7110
www.ohiocraft.org
E-mail: info@ohiocraft.org

OKLAHOMA
Oklahoma Arts Council
PO Box 52001-2001
Oklahoma City, OK 73152-2001
Phone: (405) 521-2931   Fax: (405) 521-6418
www.state.ok.us/~arts
E-mail: okarts@arts.ok.gov

OREGON
Guild of Oregon Woodworkers
PO Box 13744
Portland, OR 97218
Phone: (503) 761-0070
www.guildoforegonwoodworkers.com
info@guildoforegonwoodworkers.com

Oregon Arts Commission
775 Summer St. NE, Suite 200
Salem, OR 97310
Phone: (503) 986-0082   Fax: (503) 986-0260
www.oregonartscommission.org
E-mail: oregon.artscomm@state.or.us

Oregon Potters Association (OPA)
Phone: (503) 222-0533
www.oregonpotters.org
E-mail: Jim@oregonpotters.org

PENNSYLVANIA
Pennsylvania Council on the Arts
216 Finance Bldg.
Harrisburg, PA 17120
Phone: (717) 787-6883
www.pacouncilonthearts.org

Pennsylvania-Made Crafts, Inc.
PO Box 2
Bedford, PA 15522
Phone: (814) 623-5322

Pennsylvania Guild of Craftsmen
10 Stable Mill Trail
Richboro, PA 18954
Phone: (215) 579-5997   Fax: (215) 504-0650
www.pennsylvaniacrafts.com
E-mail: pacraft@comcat.com

RHODE ISLAND
Rhode Island State Council on the Arts
One Capitol Hill, 3rd Floor
Providence, RI 02908
Phone: (401) 222-3880   Fax: (401) 222-3018
www.arts.ri.gov
E-mail: info@arts.ri.gov

SOUTH CAROLINA
Charleston Crafts, Inc.
87 Hasell St.
Charleston, SC 29401
Phone: (843) 723-2938
www.charlestoncrafts.org
E-mail: info@charlestoncrafts.org

Clay Matters
PO Box 67
Hickory Grove, SC 29717

South Carolina Arts Commission
1800 Gervais St.
Columbia, SC 29201
Phone: (803) 734-8696   Fax: (803) 734-8526
www.state.sc.us/arts

SOUTH DAKOTA
Aberdeen Arts Council
PO Box 1751
Aberdeen, SD 57402

Beresford Arts Council
610 W. Hemlock
Beresford, SD 57004

Brandon Arts Council
PO Box 182
Brandon, SD 57005

Visual Arts Center
PO Box 984
301 S. Main Ave.
Sioux Falls, SD 57069
Phone: (605) 367-6000
www.washingtonpavilion.org

Lakota Territory Arts Council
PO Box 102
Mission, SD 57555

Madison Arts Council
1820 N. Washington Ave.
Madison, SD 57042

South Dakota Arts Council
800 Governors Dr.
Pierre, SD 57501-2294
Phone: (605) 773-3131   Fax: (605) 773-6962
www.artscouncil.sd.gov
E-mail: sdac@state.sd.us

Spearfish Arts Center
612 N. Main St.
Spearfish, SD 57783
Phone: (605) 642-7973
www.moh-scah.com
E-mail: scah@rushmore.com

Yankton Area Arts Association
GAR Gallery
PO Box 368
Yankton, SD 57078
Phone: (605) 665-9754

TENNESSEE
Five Rivers Arts & Crafts
PO Box 39
Montgomery Bell St. Park
Burns, TN 37029

Foothills Craft Guild
PO Box 5087
Oak Ridge, TN 37831
Phone: (865) 470-0669
www.foothillscraftguild.org
E-mail: fcg@foothillscraftguild.org

Tennessee Arts Commission
401 Charlotte Ave.
Nashville, TN 37243-0780
Phone: (615) 741-1701   Fax: (615) 741-8559
www.arts.state.tn.us

Tennessee Association of Craft Artists
PO Box 12006
Nashville, TN 37212-0066
Phone: (615) 385-1904   Fax: (615) 385-1909
www.tennesseecrafts.org
E-mail: taca@mindspring.com

TEXAS
Antique & Craft Guild of Alvin
PO Box 5021
Alvin, TX 77512
Phone: (281) 331-4477
www.alvinantiques.com

The Art League of Houston
1953 Montrose Blvd.
Houston, TX 77006
Phone: (713) 523-9530   Fax: (713) 523-4035
www.artleaguehouston.org
E-mail: alh@artleaguehouston.org

Lubbock Arts Alliance
2109 Broadway St.
Lubbock, TX 79401-2912
Phone: (806) 744-2787
www.lubbockarts.org
E-mail: mail@lubbockarts.org

UTAH
Utah Arts Council
617 E. South Temple St.
Salt Lake City, UT 84102
Phone: (801) 236-7555   Fax: (801) 236-7556
www.arts.utah.gov

VERMONT
Vermont Arts Council
136 State St. Drawer 33
Montpelier, VT 05602
Phone: (802) 828-3291   Fax: (802) 828-3363
www.vermontartscouncil.org
E-mail: info@vermontartscouncil.org

Vermont State Craft Center at Frog Hollow
1 Mill St.
Middlebury, VT 05753
Phone: (802) 388-3177   Fax: (802) 388-5020
www.froghollow.org
E-mail: info@froghollow.org

Vermont Crafts Council
PO Box 938
Montpelier, VT 05601
Phone: (802) 223-3380
www.vermontcrafts.com
E-mail: vt1@aol.com

VIRGINIA
Artisans Center of Virginia
601 Shenandoah Village Dr.
Waynesboro, VA 22980
Phone: (540) 943-3294   Fax: (540) 946-3296
www.virginiaartisans.org
E-mail: ACV@nexet.net

Richmond Craftsman's Guild
1812 W. Main St.
Richmond, VA 23220

Virginia Commission for the Arts
Lewis House
223 Governor St.
Richmond, VA 23219
Phone: (804) 225-3132   Fax: (804) 225-4327
www.arts.state.va.us
E-mail: arts@arts.virginia.gov

WASHINGTON
Artist Trust
1835 12th Ave.
Seattle, WA 98122-2437
Phone: (206) 467-8734   Fax: (206) 467-9633
www.artisttrust.org
E-mail: info@artisttrust.org

Washington Potters Association (WPA)
PO Box 245
Maple Valley, WA 98038
www.washingtonpotters.org

Washington State Arts Commission
PO Box 42675
711 Capitol Way S., Suite 600
Olympia, WA 98504-2675
Phone: (360) 753-3860   Fax: (360) 586-5351
www.arts.wa.gov
E-mail: info@arts.wa.gov

Association of Pacific Northwest Quilters
Phone: (206) 297-2490
www.apnq.org
E-mail: info@apnq.org

WEST VIRGINIA
Tamarack — West Virginia's Craft Center
One Tamarack Park
Beckley, WV 25801
Toll free: (888) 262-7225
www.tamarackwv.com

WISCONSIN
Appleton Arts Center
111 W. College Ave.
Appleton, WI 54911
Phone: (920) 733-4089   Fax: (920) 733-4149
www.appletonartcenter.org
E-mail: info@appletonartcenter.org

Green Lake Arts Council
PO Box 497
Green Lake, WI 54941

Midwest Art Fairs Directory
PO Box 72
Pepin, WI 54759
Phone: (612) 871-0813
www.midwestartfairs.com
E-mail: info@midwestartfairs.com

Sauk County Arts Association
PO Box 222
Baraboo, WI 53913
Phone: (608) 254-4461

Wisconsin Arts Board
101 E. Wilson St., 1st Floor
Madison, WI 53702
Phone: (608) 266-0190   Fax: (608) 267-0380
www.arts.state.wi.us
E-mail: artsboard@arts.state.wi.us

Wisconsin Center for Paper Arts
811 Williamson St.
Madison, WI 53703
Phone: (608) 284-8394
www.wibookandpaper.org
E-mail: wcpaperarts@hotmail.com

Wisconsin Designer Crafts Council
3900 W. Brown Deer Rd., Suite A
PMB 130
Milwaukee, WI 53209
www.wdcc.org

WYOMING
Wyoming Arts Council
2320 Capitol Ave.
Cheyenne, WY 82002
Phone: (307) 777-7742   Fax: (307) 777-5499
www.wyomingartscouncil.org
E-mail: ebratt@state.wy.us

b. Canada

NATIONAL
Canadian Crafts Federation
c/o Ontario Crafts Council, Designers Walk
170 Bedford Rd., Suite 300
Toronto, ON M5R 2K9
Phone: (905) 891-5928   Fax: (905) 278-6973
www.canadiancraftsfederation.ca
E-mail: info@canadiancraftsfederation.ca

ALBERTA
Alberta Craft Council
106 St., Suite 10186
Edmonton, AB T5J 1H4
Phone: (780) 488-6611   Fax: (780) 488-8855
www.albertacraft.ab.ca
E-mail: acc@albertacraft.ab.ca

BRITISH COLUMBIA
All Sooke Arts and Crafts Society
PO Box 133
Sooke, BC V0S 1N0
www.sooke.org/crafts

Crafts Association of British Columbia
1386 Cartwright St.
Vancouver, BC V6H 3R8
Phone: (604) 687-6511
Toll free: (888) 687-6511   Fax (604) 687-6711
www.cabc.net
E-mail: cabc@telus.net

The Craft Connection Co-op
441 Baker St.
Nelson, BC V1L 4H7
Phone: (250) 352-3006

Circle Craft Co-op
1666 Johnston St., Suite 1
Vancouver, BC V6H 3S4
Phone: (604) 669-8021   Fax: (604) 669-8585
www.circlecraft.net
E-mail: shop@circlecraft.net

Juan de Fuca Arts and Crafts Guild
3131 Flannagan Pl.
Victoria, BC V9B 4H2
Phone: (250) 478-8439

MANITOBA
Manitoba Crafts Council
237 McDermot Ave.
Winnipeg, MB R3B 0S4
Phone: (204) 487-6114   Fax: (204) 487-6115
www.manitobacrafts.ca
E-mail: info@manitobacrafts.ca

NEW BRUNSWICK
New Brunswick Crafts Council
PO Box 1231
87 Regent St.
Fredericton, NB E3B 5C8
Phone: (506) 450-8989
Toll free: (866) 622-7238   Fax: (506) 457-6010

NEWFOUNDLAND
Craft Council of Newfoundland and Labrador
Devon House Craft Centre
59 Duckworth St.
St. John's, NF A1C 1E6
Phone: (709) 753-2749   Fax: (709) 753-2766
www.craftcouncil.nf.ca
E-mail: info@craftcouncil.nf.ca

NOVA SCOTIA
Nova Scotia Designer Crafts Council
1113 Marginal Rd.
Halifax, NS B3H 4P7
Phone: (902) 423-3837   Fax: (902) 422-0881
www.nsdcc.ns.ca
E-mail: office@nsdcc.ns.ca

ONTARIO
Ontario Crafts Council
Designers Walk
170 Bedford Rd.
Toronto, ON M5R 2K9
Phone: (416) 925-4222   Fax: (416) 925-4223
www.craft.on.ca
E-mail: info@craft.on.ca

PRINCE EDWARD ISLAND
Prince Edward Island Council of the Arts
156 Richmond St.
Charlottetown, PE C1A 1H9
Phone: (902) 368-4410   Fax: (902) 368-4418
www.peiartscouncil.com
E-mail: info@peiartscouncil.com

QUEBEC
Conseil des Metiers d'Art du Quebec
Marche Bonsecours
350 Rue Saint-Paul Est, Suite 400
Montreal, PQ H2Y 1H2
Phone: (514) 861-2787   Fax: (514) 861-9191
www.metiers-d-art.qc.ca

SASKATCHEWAN
Saskatchewan Crafts Council
813 Broadway Ave.
Saskatoon, SK S7N 1B5
Phone: (306) 653-3616   Fax: (306) 244-2711
www.saskcraftcouncil.org
E-mail: saskcraftcouncil@shaw.ca

Appendix 3

ONLINE STORES AND MALLS

This is a sampling, generated by the major search engines, to show something of the variety of craft outlets currently on the Net. The list here is not intended to be an endorsement of any of these stores or the products displayed in them, and it is furnished on the basis and understanding that neither the author nor publisher is to be under any responsibility or liability whatsoever in respect thereof. Craftspeople looking for an online outlet should carefully consider the twelve questions discussed in Chapter 7 before making a decision about selling their work through any particular store. While the information here is current at the time of writing, it is subject to change, which is beyond the control of the author or publisher.

American Art Directory

americancraftdirectory.com/

There is a one-time set-up fee of $75.00 for up to four images and the text equivalent of one 8½" x 11" sheet of paper. Additional material may be added at a similar rate.

"You may use the URL associated with your page (www.american-craftdirectory.com/yoursitename.html) as your web address in any advertising that you do."

American Crafts Online

www.craftsonline.com

"AmericanCraftsOnline, Inc. is sponsored by Sugarloaf Mountain Works, Inc., producer of the award winning Sugarloaf Craft Festivals. For over 20 years, Sugarloaf has been presenting high-quality professional fine arts and contemporary craft festivals around the country." All work is juried. There are no set-up or monthly fees; craftspeople are charged a 20 percent commission on each sale.

CraftsCanada.com

www.craftscanada.com

"You will be able to present yourself, a description of your art, as well as a list of the craft shows you attend… Internet visitors will be able to search for craft artists by province, city, category of craft, craft show, etc." You can update information yourself on-line as many times as you want at no extra cost. There is a registration fee of $30 per year.

Craft Connections

www.craftconnections.com

An online store where for $4.95 per month you can have your own web page with 5 pictures and descriptions. Price includes a traffic counter, free Logo Header, a search feature, and a listing in the *Craft-connection* newsletter.

Craft Mall.com

www.craftmall.com

An Internet mall offering a variety of packages from $199.95 (plus $24.95 monthly) up to $679.96 (plus $ 49.95 monthly). The basic package includes: store activation and setup; up to 5 product set-ups and 5 photo scans; up to 5 image optimizations; 5 product data entries; 1 e-mail account; 1 product spotlight on Craft Mall.com main page; 1 default URL that routes directly to your store (eg., www.craft-mall.com/yourstorename/).

Coomers Craft Mall

www.coomers.com

Coomers has operated "bricks and mortar" craft stores for 12 years, "displaying only the highest quality crafts in a pleasant, department store setting and friendly sales staff." The stores sell a wide variety of crafts from home accessories to heirloom quality toys, clothing and jewelry. At the time of writing their "Global Gallery" online operation was not taking new applications but craftspeople were advised to check back at a later date.

Craftfinder.com
www.craftfinder.com

"When one of your crafts sells we send you an e-mail giving you the name and address of the person who ordered the product. We will also e-mail you a packing slip. You simply print out the packing slip, and ship the product with the packing slip enclosed, within 2 working days of receipt. On the 10th of the next month we will send you a check for 80 percent of the selling price. There is a one-time setup fee of $5 plus $5 per item."

CraftMark
www.craftmark.com

Offers three different packages, from $10 per month to $19.99 per month with a six-month contract. The basic package includes a 5 item display, e-mail link, printable order form. For an extra amount, all three packages can be customized with such options as: a visitor counter ($1 per month); automatic e-mail order form ($5 per month); secure auto e-mail form ($10 per month); additional 5 items ($5.99 per month); shopping cart ($25 per month).

Crafts Report
www.craftsreport.com

The is the Web site of the magazine *Crafts Report*. It has a "craft artist finder" section where craftspeople can offer their work for sale. For text only, there is a $25 fee per year; for text and one image, $50 per year; text and 2 images, $75 per year; text and 3 images, $95 per year; text and 4 images, $110 per year. A listing includes 25 words of descriptive text and links to e-mail and Web-site addresses.

National Craft Association
ww.craftassoc.com

Offers two packages, costing $89 and $129. Basic packages include web page design, including your company logo and full color photo (a picture of your display booth or product line), e-mail reply feature, descriptive text about your work, your contact information, and your own Internet address. Additional photos can be added for $7 each and changes in text and photos can be made for $7 each. Basic packages include hosting on the NCA Web site for one year.

Sellplace.com
www.sellplace.com

Advertises itself as a place for both "crafters and artists." Fees start at $99 for set-up, plus $5 per page. Included in this is a home page with your company logo, linked thumbnail photos, e-mail link, searchable listing, secure shopping cart with full order processing of phone, mail, and fax orders.

Wholesalecrafts.com Inc.
www.wholesalecrafts.com

One of the few online crafts wholesalers. Artists and craftspeople can present their work on this site for approximately $600 per year. There are no commissions. Buyers for retail stores and galleries can log onto the site and search for artists by a number of criteria, including name, business name, or even the craft shows they attend. There is a separate "gallery" section for artists selling work for more than $150 wholesale.